CHINA'S CRISIS, CHINA'S HOPE

LIU BINYAN

China's Crisis, China's Hope

TRANSLATED BY
HOWARD GOLDBLATT

Harvard University Press
Cambridge, Massachusetts
London, England   1990

This book is published with the assistance of the John K. Fairbank
Center for East Asian Research, Harvard University.

This book is printed on acid-free paper, and its binding materials
have been chosen for strength and durability.

Library of Congress Cataloging-in-Publication Data

Liu, Pin-yen, 1925–
    China's crisis, China's hope / Liu Binyan ; translated
by Howard Goldblatt.
        p.   cm.
    Includes index.
    ISBN 0-674-11882-0
    1. China—Politics and government—1976–   I. Title.
DS779.26.L57   1990   90-33901
951.05—dc20   CIP

In memory of Howard Simons,
who fought for freedom of the press everywhere

FOREWORD

When it was announced that Liu Binyan would speak at Harvard, in September 1988, the sense of anticipation was palpable and grew as the weeks went by. The Harvard-Yenching auditorium, which usually holds several hundred people, was already filled thirty minutes before his first lecture. People were sitting on the stairs, standing in the aisles, and kneeling on the stage, leaving just enough room for Liu and his interpreter. A fist fight broke out in the hallway as too many people tried to push into a space with no more room. Chinese and Americans came from up and down the east coast to hear Liu speak. Soon after he began to talk, someone in the audience interrupted him, asking that the translator be dispensed with so that the rhythm of his speech would not be broken. At the beginning and end of his lecture, the audience gave him a standing ovation.

Why does Liu, this writer-journalist, generate so much excitement? Born in 1925 in Changchun (Manchuria), he is regarded as China's preeminent intellectual, exemplifying in his words and actions the tradition of the courageous literati of independent conscience who criticized China's political leaders when they did not live up to their ideals. Since the beginning of China's 1949 revolution, Liu, a party member and Marxist believer, has pointed out how the Chinese Communist Party, by its abuse of power and its unresponsiveness to the demands of the ordinary people, also did not implement its ideals.

To be a principled intellectual under the Communist regime was much more difficult than under the Chinese emperors, who at times responded to criticisms from the literati. In 1957 Liu was expelled from the party and sent to the countryside to do hard physical labor. In the Cultural Revolution (1966–1976) he was incarcerated and then sent away again for reform through labor. He was unable to publish, and his family was barely able to support itself. As he has said, without the support of his caring and indomitable wife, Zhu Hong, who stood by him during two decades of ostracism and persecution, he might not have survived.

With the establishment of the Deng Xiaoping regime in late 1978 and the rehabilitation of virtually all political prisoners by Deng's protégé, Hu Yaobang, Liu was made "special correspondent" for the party's official newspaper, *People's Daily*. By 1979 he had begun an extraordinary series of investigative essays that exposed the party's corrupt practices and suppression of people's rights by party officials that continued into the Deng era. Again Liu became the subject of political campaigns, but because these campaigns were without the violence and mass participation of the Mao era, he continued to write. His exposés electrified the nation until he was purged from the party once again along with his political patron Hu Yaobang, who was dismissed as the party's general-secretary in January 1987.

Liu's views have gradually changed since the 1950s. He has moved away from the traditional Chinese reliance on ideology as a means of persuading the leadership to restrain its political power toward increasing stress on political institutions, an independent judiciary, and freedom of press to protect society from the abuses of political power. This shift of emphasis has been gradual, influenced by western ideas and Liu's stay in the west since March 1988. Most important, however, it has resulted from his and his fellow intellectuals' bitter experience at the hands of a party–government that not only was unrestrained by the intellectuals' ideological injunctions but, in fact, punished the intellectuals for their advice.

This book is based on five lectures given in the semester year of 1988–89 under the auspices of the Fairbank Center for East Asian Research. It richly details the conflict between a changing Chinese society and an unresponsive, corrupt party leadership. Liu's incisive document helps to explain what produced the explosive confrontation in Tiananmen Square in the spring of 1989 with more insight than most works written since the crackdown.

Liu cannot be compared with any writer in western countries. His position in China resembles that of the dissident East European intellectuals, such as Vaclav Havel of Czechoslovakia, who, though seemingly politically powerless, have had a profound impact on their societies, leading to the revolutions in Eastern Europe at the end of 1989. If China's leaders, like their Eastern European counterparts, had not chosen to use military force against their own citizens, who knows what position Liu might hold in his country today? Now he is in exile and excoriated by China's present leaders in their controlled media. When the time comes for these leaders to leave the scene, whether through natural or political causes, there is no question that Liu and his writings will have influenced whatever new leaders and new system may emerge. Thus this book gives us insights into China's future as well as its immediate past.

Merle Goldman

CONTENTS

PREFACE

In China very few citizens are given the opportunity of foreign travel. Only the government can grant this and other privileges (higher education, employment, housing assignments), which are reserved for those favored by the Chinese Communist Party. So in addition to being a mark of one's social standing, overseas travel also affirms the trust in which the party leadership holds an individual.

Superficially, or officially, I am not considered a hostile element, but have long been a borderline case. Thanks to the unstinting efforts of James Thomson and the late Howard Simons, the Nieman Foundation at Harvard extended me an invitation to visit the United States five times since 1983, but I was prevented from leaving each year. Then in 1988, after being expelled from the party, I was suddenly given permission to go. Since it is not in the best interests of the Chinese Communist Party to permit someone who has recently been punished for unconfessed crimes to travel to a country where he is free to speak his mind, and since it would be nearly unprecedented to give one of these plums to an incorrigible "criminal," why bestow this favor on me? In part, I think, it was an attempt to defuse public indignation and resentment, domestic and international, over the regime's more public perverse deeds. Even so trifling an incident reflects a fundamental change in China, a transformation of the role of China's people.

In a country where there are no open elections and no freedom of speech, the will of the people is virtually denied expression. In theory, since political power does not emanate from the people, they can simply be ignored. That's the way things were done during the nearly three decades of Mao Zedong's rule. But things began to change after his death, not in the legal or political system but in practical terms: after 1979, the party leaders had to begin to pay some respects to the people, even though they refuse to admit it. Lacking Mao's self-confidence, they appear to feel partly responsible for the harm their thirty-year history of blunders has inflicted on the nation. They sense a greater need to reach the hearts of the people. This can be seen by way of the three campaigns against "bourgeois liberalization" launched since 1981: each of them was brought to a screeching halt in response to popular opposition.

This does not of course mean that the Chinese Communist Party will not continue to make mistakes. The January 1987 campaign, for example, was more wanton than its two predecessors and resulted in the fall from grace of Hu Yaobang, the only party leader who enjoyed prestige among the people, and the expulsion from the party of three intellectuals who were trusted and respected by the people. This sent shock waves throughout the party and society at large, causing Deng Xiaoping's stock to plummet and shattering the people's confidence in the party. Dissension and discord within the party and Deng's clique grew more pronounced, as pessimism and despair throughout society intensified. None of this was posted or written about or made headlines, but the party sensed what was going on through its various sources. In Beijing the people had expressed discontent over the two earlier campaigns by their silence, but in this latest campaign, many complained at meetings over the punishment meted out to the four people, calling the Central Committee of the party to account. This had never happened before, and even in conservative provincial places like Yantai, Hangzhou, and Taiyuan large posters and handbills appeared.

On a sweltering night in July 1957, at a general meeting of *China Youth Daily* workers, I was publicly labeled an antiparty, antisocial rightist, after which everyone stopped speaking to me. But on the afternoon of January 24, 1987, as news of my expulsion from the party was broadcast on radio and television, no fewer than twenty-seven people, most of whom I barely knew, came to my home to comfort and encourage me. Even before the official announcement, I had received sympathetic telephone calls, telegrams, letters, and visitors, some of whom invited me to take refuge in their homes. Kindhearted readers began sending me food, medicine, cash, and health products. It was an interesting development, for these people all felt that I had suffered from being kicked out of the party, not realizing that their good wishes were gains that far outweighed my losses, if indeed I had lost anything.

Since it was difficult for me to go out during this time, I received regular visits from a few good friends who brought me encouraging news in spite of the prospect of being observed or overheard by the secret police. But my friends were worried about China's future, convinced there was no way to change oppressive policies; some even believed that a period like the Brezhnev era that had gripped the Soviet Union for eighteen years was beginning in China. But I took the opposite view, consoling them by saying, "It won't happen. Small changes will occur within six months, great ones within three years." Events proved me right. In his speech of May 13, Zhao Ziyang brought a halt to the campaign against bourgeois liberalization; two years and three months later, the 1989 democracy movement erupted in Tiananmen Square.

It is difficult for people sizing up politics to break the habit of keeping their eyes focused on the top. In China, that may have been all right prior to 1966, but since the outbreak of the Cultural Revolution, and especially since the implementation of economic reforms, the party's control over Chinese society has grown increasingly slack; the distance between what the party leadership wants to do and what it is capable of doing has grown considerably. The atmosphere of concern, anxiety, and fear among the old men in Zhongnanhai has become more palpable than ever before. China's political system has made it necessary for actual situations to be revealed only in an indirect manner, so there is always more to matters than meets the eye. News blackouts make it impossible for people to be aware of significant events, even those close to home. And ever since 1979, when great changes began to occur in China, intellectuals have had less and less contact with China's realities. Although there have been numerous expositions on Mao Zedong's views of the role of the masses in our history, in fact he saw them as mere tools of class struggle and economic production. His pronouncements that intellectuals must unite with the workers and peasants served his greater purpose of oppressing those same intellectuals.

The popular ideological trends of the 1980s are diametrically opposed to the extremist ideology under Mao, having moved to another extreme. Back then, politics was everything; now it is nothing. Back then, "serve the people" was the essential revolutionary slogan; now disdaining the people is considered progressive. Back then, to advocate "work only for the people, not for oneself" was the norm, even if those who shouted it the loudest actually did the opposite; now it has become fashionable to advocate "work only for oneself, not for the people." Back then, intellectuals were to go among the masses; now they are permitted to live comfortably and in good conscience in their own closed circles.

We now enjoy the previously denied opportunity and freedom

to study foreign countries, but in this surge of study, even imitation, China's realities have somehow been lost from view, just when the nation is experiencing earth-shaking changes everywhere. Millions of peasants have been released from their slavery, suddenly granted for the first time in thirty years the freedom to work their own fields, perform any labor they please, even engage in commerce; for the first time they are free to travel wherever they choose. Never before have there been such intense changes in their feelings and moods, their desires and thoughts, their courage, or their attitudes toward people and events. The consciousness of being a human being that lay dormant in the hearts of hundreds of millions of people has been stirred. But along with the desire to be productive and creative has come a frenzied desire to possess and enjoy things; along with courage, diligence, and a sense of revival have come greed and cruelty. Fierce struggles against the old power bases have begun breaking out in the cities and the countryside.

My job as a reporter and the choices I made in what I wrote presented me with opportunities to maintain contact with people from all levels of Chinese society. Since 1979 I have been haunted by a feeling that the tide of reform engulfing the lower levels of society is eroding the foundations of this unique empire. I often speak of two processes in motion at the same time, one a system of organized economic reforms originating in the Central Committee, the other a series of great spontaneous transformations going on at the lower levels of society and spreading into every facet of the people's lives. The latter changes are far more profound than the former, since they involve the people's economic status, political situation, lifestyles, interpersonal relationships, modes of thinking, and ethical values. These are the forces that will someday determine the future of China; right now they cannot fail to exert a powerful influence on Chinese society and on the Communist Party.

Comparing the period 1949–1966 to 1979–1988, one is struck by a sharp difference. In almost every one of the seventeen years between Liberation and the Cultural Revolution, Mao Zedong launched some sort of political or economic campaign in which the people were relegated to minor roles, forever "supporting enthusiastically" and "responding to the call," paying the price day after day in total disregard of their own safety (even of their own lives), until the campaign had run its course and they were left to pick up the pieces. But all that changed after the Cultural Revolution.

Since 1949, all mass movements and demonstrations in China were carefully organized by the Communist Party. In the Tiananmen Incident of 1976 the Chinese people mounted the stage of history as principal actors for the first time. On April 5th, the traditional day for commemorating the dead, thousands gathered in Tiananmen Square to express dissatisfaction with the Gang of Four, through speeches, poems, and garlands. It was a peaceful and spontaneous demonstration, harshly repressed by the regime. This was followed by what came to be called the

Democracy Wall Movement. At the end of 1978 the third plenum of the Chinese Communist Party, reversing the practice of Chairman Mao, decided to advocate economic reform. At the same time, a group of young people started to post big-character posters at the Xidan Intersection in Beijing, demanding not only economic reform but democracy and political reform as well. Their outstanding leader was Wei Jingsheng, who was later sentenced to fifteen years and is still in prison.

Signs of popular unrest continued, and in 1980 student representatives were elected to the District People's Congress on university campuses in Beijing, Shanghai, and a few other places. All these activities were carried out by the people independently, in defiance of the will of the party. In response, the Central Committee felt compelled to launch its 1981–1987 campaigns against bourgeois liberalization; these were quite unlike Mao's in that his were primarily intended to further his own ambitions. The new campaigns were deep-seated efforts intended to restrict the expansion of the people's freedom and to eliminate their role in historical measures launched by the party. The nationwide student demonstrations of 1985 and 1986 were the people's response to the two antiliberalization campaigns of 1981 and 1983.

The third campaign against bourgeois liberalization, a mammoth endeavor by the Central Committee, also failed to take the fight out of the people. In fact, it had the opposite result, for the people openly expressed opposition and journalists demanded greater freedom of the press. Work slowdowns and labor strikes increased. Hundreds of thousands of peasants in Shandong's Cangshan county rose up in protest against economic losses they had suffered at the hands of the government, and they destroyed the offices of the local government and party committee. In the city of Yueyang in Hunan province, the people organized two days of mass demonstrations to protest the unwarranted firing of a vice-mayor by a number of corrupt local party officials.

All this sheer vitality of Chinese society over the past decade stands in stark contrast to the eighteen years of Brezhnev's rule in the Soviet Union and the two decades of inactivity after the 1968 invasion of Czechoslovakia. Following the death of Stalin in 1953, a tide of introspection and criticism swept across the Soviet Union, and after the political shakeup of 1964, underground publications were allowed to disseminate their views for a while. Nationalistic contradictions between the countries of Eastern Europe and the Soviet Union intensified popular awakenings. A different scenario was being played out in China. The considerable prestige of the Chinese Communist Party was established largely as a result of its contribution in gaining national independence, unifying the country, and raising its international status. Yet up to 1979 not a single book, newspaper, or article described the true course of events after 1949 or the actual circumstances of the people. After 1979, and especially after 1981, the efforts of China's writers and scholars to expand the publishing market in the face of resistance to commercialism, and to promote the introduction of rudimentary democratic education among the broad masses, were clearly inadequate. But the 1985 TV dramatic series "New Star" and the 1988 documentary series "River Elegy"—which were seen as open criticism of conservative hardliners within the party—reverberated throughout Chinese society, proving that intellectuals were capable of doing a great deal more than they had done so far.

The conclusions I draw from all this, therefore, do not seem to me simplistic. In general terms, the principal force in awakening the people and setting them on the road to protest over the past forty years has been the repeated mistakes of the Chinese Communist Party and the ubiquitous corruption it has proved powerless to contain. That is why the course of this awakening has been so difficult and so tortuous. In recent years the stirring of the Chinese people has made it impossible for the rulers to enjoy a moment's peace, and it is getting worse for them every year. The final recourse was the establishment of martial law in the nation's capital.

The greatest mockery of all is that on the eve of the 1989 democracy movement, a "new authoritarianism" was sweeping across the mainland, promoted not only by Zhao Ziyang's minions but by reporters and writers who had always been considered progressive. This should not surprise us, since from 1981 to 1988, as contradictions and crises within Chinese society reached a fever pitch and protests against the Communist regime in cities and the countryside were spreading rapidly, bureaucrats and some intellectuals were bitterly complaining about how backward the Chinese people were, about the lack of conditions for democracy and how no one was doing anything to improve the situation. Countless novels were published during this period, but precious few were written for ordinary readers; great quantities of domestic and foreign works on philosophy and the social sciences appeared, but almost none of them could speak to the general reader. The scholars agreed that it was important to instruct China's masses, but the only ones who understood what they wrote were other scholars, who didn't need the instruction. Most people never heard the rumblings that signaled the events of 1989, or assumed they were too distant and indistinct to be of any real significance, so of course they were unprepared.

Realizing the limitations to my direct knowledge of Chinese society, I grew uneasy, and on the eve of my departure for the United States in 1988, I started having second thoughts about going. If political conditions had been right at the time, I would have preferred to move to the countryside for a few years. I still look forward to the day when I can return and realize this wish, for in the final analysis China's future will be determined by changes that occur in the two thousand rural counties on the mainland.

Since arriving in the United States in 1988, I have spoken at more than forty colleges and universities. I condensed the central issues of these hundred or so talks for five speeches at Harvard's John K. Fairbank Center for East Asian Research; these

form the substance of this book. Never forgetting that my workplace is in China, I must be careful to ensure that my right to
speak out is not taken away if I return to China; that is why I
have been temperate in my comments. I have mapped out my
future plans: I shall dedicate myself to analyzing the real problems China faces in a practical and realistic fashion, without
voicing opinions on the leaders of China's parties. The year
1988 saw China become engulfed in runaway inflation and accel-
erated political crises; it was also a year when the people's frus-
tration with the Communist Party and their despair for the future
reached epidemic proportions. Yet when I spoke with American
sinologists, I discovered that some of them still talk happily about
China's economic reforms and the contributions of Deng Xiaoping, paying scant attention to the dangers besetting Chinese
society and those very reforms. They seem to believe that China's
reforms have a better chance of succeeding than the Soviet
Union's perestroika. Some university audiences have felt that I
am painting too bleak a picture of the situation in China, while
overseas Chinese students sometimes accuse me of painting too
rosy a picture. They have urged me not to place hope in certain
members of the Chinese Communist Party and implied that,
unless I state that the situation is hopeless and that every member of the Communist Party is unspeakable, I will be doing the
party a favor or, worse, letting it off the hook, even selling out.

During my talks at American colleges and universities, I
often said that we could expect something astonishing to occur

at any time which would capture the attention of the entire world. I never dreamed that a democracy movement of such incredible proportions would erupt within a year. I gave my final speech at Harvard exactly two days before the death of Hu Yaobang, and there is no mention in the five essays of the 1989 Beijing democracy movement or of the party octagenarians. This must be viewed as a defect in a book published in 1990, after the unprecedentedly heroic events of last year. So I have added two essays and this preface, all written after the June Fourth massacre, to make up for the deficiency. "Deng's Pyrrhic Victory" was published first in *The New Republic*, October 2, 1989, as translated by Corinna-Barbara Francis; some revisions have been made for this book.

January 1990   Liu Binyan
Hartford, Connecticut

CHINA'S CRISIS,
CHINA'S HOPE

China is unique. Not only is it different from western countries, but there are major differences between it and the Soviet Union and Eastern Europe. For one thing, much of China's history over the past four thousand years, including major events, is not clearly understood today, even by Chinese. Large numbers of people are not even aware of major events occurring now. In a 1984 speech in China I advocated a policy of openness, saying that it would be better to expose, rather than conceal, the various contradictions in Chinese society. A year later, Soviet President Mikhail Gorbachev introduced glasnost, which was what I was talking about. Obviously China and the Soviet Union have much in common. But there are differences too. The implementation of glasnost in the Soviet Union led to an expansion of freedom of the press and breakthroughs in political reform. But even though China is more advanced in introducing economic reforms, not only has there not been a corresponding expansion in freedom of the press, but it actually shrank during the 1980s. Characteristic of China in recent decades has been that certain events are revealed through the progress of history rather than by official announcements. History is our spokesman and the means by which the people learn the true facts. The runaway inflation on the China mainland occurring now constitutes one of these historical revelations.

According to official statistics, from 1985 to 1987 the rate of inflation was 10–20 percent. But people in urban centers felt it was much higher. In 1985 I sensed that residents of Beijing and

3

other cities were fed up with the rising cost of living, and worried that there might be an incident, for the inflation came just when the people were fed up with the failures of the party and its rampant corruption. The budget deficit announced by the government was probably half the true figure, and the same ratio probably existed between the announced and true rate of inflation, which for some consumer goods doubled between 1985 and 1987. By 1985 I knew that the people's savings were melting away like an ice cube, as the interest rate continued to lag behind inflation. Yet it never occurred to depositors, in their innocence, to withdraw their savings and invest them in goods.

But the day of reckoning came in the spring of 1988, as panic set in among residents of China's cities, who feared that the ice cube was about to evaporate altogether. In Beijing the panic probably began at the beginning of the year, when pork and egg rationing was restored. That was followed by skyrocketing prices for essential nonstaple foods and, during March and April, panic buying of items like matches, toilet paper, soap, and salt; the situation quickly spread to other cities and has been repeated off and on ever since. Since August 1988 there has also been panic buying of durable goods. Television sets, refrigerators, washing machines, air conditioners, expensive cameras, and tape recorders, regardless of brand name, where they were made, or quality, have all been disappearing from the shelves. There have been cases of people buying ten washing machines and two refrigerators; one family bought two adult bicycles for their seven-year-old daughter, one to use when she entered high school and one for her dowry. Some people have bought enough matches to last them twenty years, and shops have sold as much salt in one day as they used to sell in a month. For some it is a matter of stocking up on consumable items, but for people who buy a ton of salt, there is clearly another purpose. They are converting their cash (*renminbi* or RMB) into goods that will hold their price, making these goods a form of savings. The summer and fall witnessed runs on banks all over China. People began lining up at the crack of dawn, forcing some banks to place limits on withdrawals. People who had never once lost faith in the Chinese Communist Party and its currency began to withdraw their savings and convert them into goods or exchange them for American dollars on the black market at twice or three times the official rate.

Many Chinese are in a state of shock: after forty years of party rule, they are for the first time beginning to doubt its authority and ability to control the economy; their confidence is being eroded. And they are surprised to find how many other people share this attitude.

People may recall the final year of Guomindang rule forty years ago, when staggering inflation caused panic among the people and a frenzy of buying. Of course there are major differences. In 1948, the country was engulfed in a civil war, and Communist troops were in control of nearly all the countryside and most of the cities. The worst inflation occurred in coastal cities, caused in large part by the Communist troops, who cut off the supply of goods from the countryside and areas under their control, starting with grain and nonstaple goods. But we have enjoyed nearly forty years of peace, and there are no enemy forces on the mainland capable of creating economic havoc. Back then, economic power rested with private individuals, and now it is largely in government hands. Back then, many anti-Guomindang student strikes broke out in the cities, but, as I speak, all is quiet. Back then, panic was inevitable, given the ever-present dangers of starvation and the collapse of the government, which would make its currency worthless. Neither of these conditions exists now, and yet the panic atmosphere is strikingly similar to that of those earlier days. Why?

One can say with confidence that virtually none of China's citizens has any understanding of the causes or effects of the current inflationary spiral. The government finds it unnecessary to inform the people of economic difficulties and problems, concentrating instead on making sure they regularly hear about all the joyous events that go on. Almost no one believes that the Chinese Communist Party will lose its grip on power; in fact, the panic and depression spreading across the country are tied to the very realization that the government will not collapse and the belief that the party and the government will not undergo any changes. This political power was wrested away from the corrupt Guomindang regime two generations ago by the people, who joyously welcomed the party to their cities. But now they are agonizing over their inability to make it go away and the fact that there is nothing in the wings to replace it.

Meanwhile, the mood of the people shows that inflation is not just an economic issue, but a distinctly political one. Almost every article in print and conference report on inflation touches upon the issue of the budget deficit: the deficit is growing annually, the only remedy at hand is to print more currency, and this is a direct cause of inflation. Where does all the money go? Of the more than 200 billion yuan in government expenditures, one third goes to subsidies for money-losing state enterprises and price subsidies for food and goods necessary to the people.

A third of the industry built up over more than thirty years of "socialist planned economy" lies idle. Twenty percent of the operational enterprises lose money and must be supported, in full or in part, by the national government. More and more are having to shut down operations two or three days a week, sometimes more, owing to shortages in energy and raw materials or difficulties in transportation; originally operating in the black, in recent years they have joined the ranks of subsidized enterprises. Lacking social-security insurance and unemployment benefits, the workers in nonoperational factories must be subsidized if they are to survive. Then there are the millions of potentially unemployed in operating factories who fill redundant jobs. Figures cannot do justice to the nationwide problem of high consumption and low efficiency, but it occurs all the time, in every department and enterprise, and in the lives of every worker.

In the past ten years, all sorts of methods have been tried in order to breathe new life into the moribund economy: added powers and responsibilities to management personnel in enterprises to spark initiative; increased benefits to workers in order to stimulate enthusiasm. Nothing has worked. The consensus in economic and intellectual circles seems to be that the system of ownership must be overhauled and that China must move from a system of "ownership by the whole people" to one of collective or individual ownership—in other words, real owners.

But this proposal is constantly attacked or impeded by high-ranking conservative elements in the party. One of the goals of the three "antibourgeois" campaigns from 1981 to 1987 has been to stifle economic reforms and return to pre-1966 policies, what they refer to as true socialism. They label the ten years of reform as bourgeois liberalization, the first step in a return to capitalism.

Conservative elements within the party represent the interests of the bureaucracy, and inflation, like so many of China's problems, is heavily political in nature. The devaluation of RMB is an indication of problems accumulated since the implementation of economic reforms over the past decade. It is both an economic and a political issue, which exposes the impotence of the government and the corruption of the Communist Party. One can nearly see the expression of the Chinese people in their currency. Their deflated spirit, their sagging morale, their grave disappointment, and their mood of dejection are all expressed in China's devalued currency.

The crux of China's problems lies in its vast bureaucracy and privileged class. This clique was exposed by intellectuals in 1956 and 1957. Although these critics gave China a golden opportunity, they were crushed by the bureaucrats. Several more opportunities were lost over the thirty years that followed. The bureaucratic clique has such strength that even the Cultural Revolution could not eliminate it; if anything, it has become stronger. I can't say with precision how large the bureaucracy is, but figures show how its numbers have swelled. In a 1957 talk Mao Zedong said that 1.8 million cadres were on the public payroll; a document in my possession in 1984 showed that the number was 6.4 million. By 1986 this number had swelled to 12 million, although one source gives it as 27 million. I believe that even this is a conservative figure.

In recent years, China's senior leaders have frequently commented that the economies of Asia's "Four Little Dragons" (Taiwan, Hong Kong, South Korea, and Singapore) have prospered without any form of democratization—so why must China promote democratization? But this ignores the factor of the 12 million people who handle China's economic lifeline, who control over 90 percent of the economy. They can use their power to gain personal benefits without fear of punishment and are free to make mistakes and never suffer the consequences, no matter how much damage they cause. Where would Taiwan or Korea be if it had to support these lords and masters? The representatives of this clique have opposed Deng Xiaoping's economic reforms since 1978, even though, ironically, these reforms have brought them enormous benefits.

To begin with, the reforms have led to a considerable expansion of government agencies, particularly those involved with economics. A few statistics will illustrate this. A company in Guangzhou decided to build a factory; after sixteen months of administrative formalities, a total of 571 official stamps had been obtained, each representing a separate bureau, and 424 more were still required. Since some people doubted the accuracy of these figures, *People's Daily* reported another example, of a planned hydroelectric plant in Hunan for which 1,460 official stamps were required; the documents and construction plans weighed 170 kilograms, and final approval came two and a half years later. These figures illustrate the parasitic nature of the bureaucracy. The point of its existence has little to do with its functions in society, but is limited to its own perpetuation. These people need not be concerned with efficiency or ability; the political and economic systems free them from any repercussions that would threaten their well-fed existence.

The salaries for 12–27 million bureaucrats constitute a heavy drain on the government's budget. But salary alone is not the reason they live so well. The primary cause of China's inflation is the so-called buying power of social groups, unique to China.

This means that the government pays for the expenses of party organs, government agencies, state-controlled companies and enterprises, and many state-subsidized social organizations. These are fixed expenditures, and every year there are repeated calls to control the consumption of the social groups, but it increases every year. In 1977, total consumption was 13.4 billion yuan; in 1986 the figure was 46.2 billion, and in 1987 it jumped to 55.3 billion. This included great quantities of high-quality consumer items (high-quality by Chinese standards). In 1986, 760,000 foreign automobiles were imported, at a cost of 5.2 billion U.S. dollars, a figure that includes not only the cost of the automobiles but maintenance costs as well (4.7 yuan equal 1 U.S. dollar). The buying power of social groups constitutes 10 percent of the cost of consumer goods of society at large, therefore contributing to soaring prices and runaway inflation; moreover, these people demand hard-to-get, expensive goods.

Officials who control China's economy, from the premier, vice-premiers, ministers and commissioners (most of China's ministries have economic management responsibilities), leaders of provincial and municipal departments and bureaus, even factory managers and section chiefs, all possess economic powers without the commensurate responsibilities. I cannot recall hearing of any high or mid-level official being held legally responsible for mistaken economic policies or any low-level official being held liable for economic losses stemming from dereliction of duty. Economic development, moreover, is primarily tied to an increase in the total value of production, which works to both the material and the political advantage of officials. So even though there has been a call every year, going back to Mao's era, for cutbacks, capital construction has increased rather than decreased. Every province, every municipality, even the leadership of the central government, has a vested interest in seeing production increase in its own backyard: it enhances their reputation and lengthens their political life, and it enlarges their power base, which in turn brings additional benefits, such as increased local revenues, greater employment opportunities, access to national energy and material resources, products to exchange with other locales, and more.

From the early 1950s through the late 1970s, a period of almost thirty years, production in China's state-run economy was not geared to the market or, for that matter, to the needs of the people. Rather it was centered on fulfilling state plans, production for the sake of production, so that a significant characteristic of the "socialist" economy was its self-perpetuating growth. From the beginning it showed a hunger for investment: without an expansion of industrial construction, how could the increasing amounts of iron and steel, machine tools, and raw materials be consumed? And the result of an expansion of industrial capacity was that more and more new products were used in industrial construction. As time passed, a sort of inertia developed, until even revenues were dependent upon the rate of increase of industrial development. Today there are many areas where, unless there is an annual increase of 20–30 percent, the quality of life suffers badly, to the point where salaries for local officials are held up. Already there is a surplus of productive capacity in existing factories, but new ones are built: raw materials are not forthcoming and no products reach the market, so they must cease production. But even though they operate at a loss, no harm is done, for they can rely upon bank loans or subsidies from the state to stay in existence. Year in and year out, vast quantities of state funds, construction materials, and raw materials are invested in new construction sites and factories. In 1987, the outlay for capital construction exceeded that of the previous year by 34 percent, a total of 124 billion yuan; 40 percent of this money had been earmarked for extra wages to be paid to the workers in these newly constructed enterprises, which stimulated consumer markets.

The reckless pursuit of production output has already become an incurable symptom of China's state-run economy, as in the Soviet Union. China's factories are producing items unwanted in the marketplace or whose quality does not conform to the needs of the consumers, so these goods simply pile up in warehouses. The overstocked goods from China's heavy and light industries have a total value of 66.7 billion yuan. What this means is that year after year huge sums of the people's hard-earned money must be diverted to subsidize a vast army of cadres and workers to produce goods that no one wants.

But these economic wastes do not adequately explain why the

Chinese national treasury is so empty. Economic construction is now in its fourth decade, reforms have been in place for ten years, and production is increasing annually, or so the newspapers tell us. The money is going to the cliques I referred to earlier, for it is they who control every segment of our political and economic lives, relying in large part on their private monopoly of the most desperately needed goods and materials. Recently newspapers have been exposing incidents of "bureauprof," bureaucratic profiteering. This is but a new term for something that has been going on for years; only the scope of the problem is new, and it is political as well as economic. Even though people have been exposing these practices and appealing to the authorities since 1979, their opposition has not led to any reduction of this illegal activity for private gain. On the contrary, it is worse than ever, for now that it has gone public, it has become a vast, open, completely legal phenomenon. Allow me to cite one example.

Nearly 10 percent of China's population lives below the poverty level, scarcely able to keep body and soul together. The problem of survival for these people remains unsolved. Most of them live in the soviet areas established over half a century ago, where the Communist Party had its roots. I spent a year doing manual labor in one of these rural areas in 1958, so I know the situation well. Pingshun is an impoverished county in the Taihang mountain region of Shanxi, and in the village where I was working, there was no water anywhere, neither subterranean nor from rivers, so it relied solely upon rainwater stored in a large pond. The county is so poor that annual revenues do not exceed 2 million yuan. But expenditures total 12 million a year. The additional 10 million comes from government subsidies. Impoverished counties throughout China all rely upon subsidies from the government in Beijing. In any comparison between the mainland and Taiwan, this situation must be factored in. There would be no problem if the 12 million in expenditures were reasonable. But in Pingshun county, where the people don't have enough food to eat or clothes to keep warm, over 150 automobiles were imported. And the purchase price was no mere drop in the bucket; a car that originally cost 30,000–50,000 yuan was bought for 130,000–140,000, with maintenance and fuel adding 10,000 more.

This is not an isolated case. If you travel to any county in China, even in the poorest you will be struck by the splendor of the government buildings, with their assembly halls and guest houses. Not only are the county committee and county government housed in imposing edifices, but every bureau has a building of its own, not to mention spacious compounds and living quarters. Every bureau also has a separate guest house. Even the family-planning offices are located in separate buildings. State funds are sent to these impoverished counties every year to help increase production, buy grain, and build homes: allowances for the poor, they are called. The money gets skimmed off at the county level, and then again at the district and village levels.

Go to one of the villages and ask a peasant what he gets. He'll tell you that he signed a paper a couple of years ago for 500 yuan, which he never got, then signed a paper last year for 300 yuan, which he never got. In places like this, the party branch secretary and the village chief have fine houses. Some of the district chiefs take the state subsidies—the peasants' money—and buy land in the county seat to build two-story villas, many with large enclosed courtyards. Some live there themselves, others rent them out. The bureaucrats have become unbelievably rapacious.

In the past, officials certainly used their authority for personal economic advantage, but their acquisitions were considered illegal; the harm they inflicted on society by misappropriating state funds and diverting the public wealth within the scope of their duties was more or less indirect. But the problem that surfaced in 1988 was of a vastly different nature. The bureaucrats and their relatives were diverting public funds through the authority of party organizations to enter the realm of production and commodities by setting up state-funded companies; their speculation and profiteering caused untold damage to the national economy as they reaped staggering profits. To illustrate: one of the most serious problems facing China today is the energy shortage; an inadequate transportation system has led to huge stockpiles of coal at the mine sites, where there is always the danger of spontaneous combustion. Owing to this inability to supply approved customers from the stockpiles of coal produced in accordance with state plans, "bureauprof" companies pay the asking price for means of transportation, then ship the coal on national railroads or in government-owned trucks to the coastal provinces and sell it there. The military uses its own trucks to ship the coal long distances for profit. This has caused the price of coal to jump from 30 or 40 yuan at the mine site to 200 or 300 at the other end. In Zhejiang province alone, the added expense for this coal is 2 billion yuan a year. The price of nonferrous aluminum, electrolytic copper, and zinc has also shot up more than twofold as a result of monopolies and speculation. China's largest producer of aluminum products, the Tianjin factory, has already stopped production for want of raw materials.

Such situations have created basic threats to the economic reforms. One of the goals is the establishment of a commodity economy with a mechanism for free competition. Competition is, of course, a good thing. The problem in China is that competition is unfair. The bureaucrats, their relatives, their sons and daughters, enjoy considerably more advantages than ordinary citizens, and it is impossible to compete with them on an equal footing. And competition is anything but free. Chinese officials make things extremely difficult for private industrialists, by bullying and even blackmailing them. It has become so bad that factory heads and managers of successful enterprises are selling their factories and getting out of the business altogether. Even more common is the arrest of industrialists and reformers, who are sentenced to prison terms after long investigations.

It should be obvious that if these "bureauprof" groups are not supervised and restricted, ultimately abolished, China's economic reforms stand no chance of success. Unhappily, the economic reforms are having no impact at all on these bureaucrats. We must give credit to Deng Xiaoping and others for initiating the reforms in 1978–79, realizing how much opposition there was from so many hardliners, high and low. The majority of provincial leaders opposed the production-responsibility system in the villages. In provinces like Guangxi in the south and Heilongjiang in the north, implementation of the system was delayed until 1983, four long years.

Many have felt that focusing only on economic reform is a mistake. The strategy of certain high-ranking individuals is clear: "We don't want to hear your opinions. Give us the peace and quiet we need to get the economy moving. Once the economy is on track, the other problems will take care of themselves." What they say makes some sense. Still, when you don't work on political reforms at the same time, economic reforms are blocked at every step. One opportunity after another has been lost for this very reason. In 1980, Deng Xiaoping solemnly announced reforms in China's political system. A directive from the Central Committee was promulgated that same year setting regulations within the party, comprised of twelve demands on all cadres, relating to political and economic issues; we call them the Twelve Articles. But both directives came to nothing. The party rectification began in 1980 when more than two hundred party members gathered in Beijing, to look into the housing conditions of senior members; those living in better quarters than they deserved would be forced to evacuate them. After three months, who did they find? First was Qiao Guanhua, who had already been removed from office and was under investigation. Next was Wang Hairong (Mao's niece). The third individual was in the same category, although I forget just who it was. All empty talk! As far as we knew, there were plenty of military people living in quarters that far exceeded the standards. Some occupied over a hundred rooms, but no one dared try to get them to move.

A wonderful slogan appeared in 1981—"Build a highly democratic and highly civilized new China." I recall seeing a banner with those words hanging above the grand auditorium in the Great Hall of the People. Later on, the words "highly democratic" disappeared; democracy was apparently no longer needed. The words became a "spiritual civilization" comprised of the "five stresses [on civilized behavior, decorum, hygiene, discipline, and morals], the four points of beauty [the mind, language, behavior, and the environment], and the three deep loves [for the motherland, socialism, and the party]."

In 1983, the launching of a thorough rectification of the party was formally announced. Many people invested considerable hope in this, since corruption within the party was clearly out of control. The lengthy resolution on party reform that emerged was a good document, and it was promoted on a grand scale for a year. But after the year was up, we looked back and were deeply saddened when we realized that it had been a year of going through the motions, nothing more. In October 1983, simultaneous with the announcement that party rectification was to begin, strangely enough another campaign was launched, to eliminate "spiritual pollution." This was very much like the antirightist campaign that preceded party rectification in 1957: first attack the rightists, then reform the party. A newspaper report announced the expulsion of 100,000 members of various ranks who had violated party laws and discipline or who had committed errors. In all, some 150,000 party members were disciplined during the party rectification, a far cry from what was going on in the Soviet Union. I don't know the number of party members in the USSR, but the figure is nowhere near China's 46 million, not among a Soviet population of 240 million. Yet Gorbachev disciplined 500,000 party members in a single year, including party secretaries and ministers of the republics as well as some ministers of the Central Committee. Even Brezhnev's son-in-law was interrogated, and a number of people were executed. I can recall the execution of only one such person in China, the head of Haifeng county, and that was in 1980, before the rectification campaign started. Newspaper reports underscored the fact that, of the 100,000 people expelled, some thirty held the rank of municipal cadre—there were no municipal party secretaries, certainly no one from the provincial level, and absolutely none at the Central Committee level. Many were like me, people who had written exposés or petitioned the Central Committee or the courts for redress of problems within the party. There were so many complaints that officials appealed to the Central Committee, accusing the masses of ideological weakness that was making their work impossible. Whenever this kind of accusation emerged, the Central Committee quickly sided with the officials, saying that we are supposed to unite in accordance with the wishes of the Central Committee and work peacefully together for "the Four Modernizations." Stability and unity are certainly necessary, but the problem is, what kind of stability and what kind of unity? Is China stable now, or unified? Forget for a moment any subjective view of the desirability of stability and unity in working peacefully for the nation's economic modernization; in objective terms, the government is turning a blind eye to the criminal misdeeds of the bureaucracy.

Problems within the bureaucracy are by no means restricted to economics. Take the case of Wang Shouxin, the subject of my 1979 piece in *People's Literature*, "Between Men and Monsters." By then this was the largest case of corruption anywhere in the country, but the monetary loss was only 480,000 RMB. Recently it was reported that one man lost the equivalent of 160,000 U.S. dollars in one night at the gambling table, without a change in facial expression. Think what that amount of corruption means! The criminals in this private-interest group infringe upon human rights by arresting people, beating them up, and throwing them in jail. There are many such cases reported in the newspapers. There was a recent story of a teacher beaten to death, accused of stealing the equivalent of a nickel. In my home county of Linyi in Shandong province, at least one person is beaten to death every year. We can raise our voices or pick up our pens to protest such incidents, but it makes no difference. Human life is valued cheaply, and violations are ignored.

The biggest problem we face today in China is not commodity prices or the cost of living. This is not to say that we don't have serious economic problems. Last year or the year before, if a family had to spend 70 or 80 percent of their income for food, now they may have to spend all of it and still come up short. I took a survey in the fall of 1987 in which I discovered that a family of three in Beijing earning under 200 yuan (about $50) a month has trouble getting by. And many couples earn only about 150 a month. The situation has worsened considerably since prices began to soar in 1988. Older couples with an income of 300–400 a month are having trouble making ends meet and have to dip into their savings just to get by.

But to my mind the most serious problem is the widespread spiritual malaise among people from all walks of life, a growing mood of depression, even despair, a loss of hope for the future and of any sense of social responsibility, as if China were no longer their country and society owed them something. I haven't seen this sort of attitude before, at least not in the past forty years. And there is no solution in sight. The malaise has already led to several minor disturbances, including dozens of labor strikes, all too small in scope to be of a specifically political nature. The most common expression of dissatisfaction and resentment by the people is a work slowdown. I am reminded of the major disturbance that followed the Great Leap Forward and the people's communes in 1958. How did the peasants express their dissatisfaction back then? By stealing. They felt they had been cheated and taken advantage of by their own government. They lost the land that had been given to them, their livestock, and even their workpoints. Instead of demonstrating in the streets, they began stealing. In recent years this has been spreading to the factories, which began to experience thefts, some quite serious. Before long, bands of people were carrying out major thefts. In 1988, in a township in Guizhou province, thefts of grain were carried out steadily for a month, at first only at night but soon in broad daylight; thefts turned into looting. The peasants in that region no longer recognized any authority. Mines were pillaged, metals were stolen, and sunken boats were scavenged by large groups of people who dredged them up, removed all the metal, and carried it back to their homes. In this respect, the relationship between the Chinese people and the Communist Party differs from that between the Soviet people and their party. The generation of people who benefited from Mao's policies were either still around or fresh in their children's memories: we are a family liberated by the Communist Party, and it was the Communist Party that put us on our feet. People were not unaware of the suffering subsequently endured under the party, but to this day the Chinese Communist Party retains a by no means small measure of its former prestige. I often say that the Chinese Communist Party has enjoyed a degree of moral authority unmatched by any other regime in the country's history. Even though people constantly witness the misdeeds of party members, they continue to view the party in a good light. Concepts, particularly traditional ones, have a powerful hold. So when people talk about forming another political party in China or setting up a multiple-party system, I think the time is not yet ripe for that.

The party of Mao Zedong devoted more effort to remolding the people's ideology and educating them in political issues than did Stalin's party. That, with all the long years of totalitarian rule, should explain why there are no underground newspapers or periodicals and no popular political organizations. This state of affairs is related to the firm ideological control of the Chinese Communist Party and China's history of literary inquisitions. Underground periodicals existed in the Soviet Union during the eighteen years of the Brezhnev era, and there are currently 30,000 popular organizations there. Of course, not all are political organizations; they include fishing and hunting clubs. But even if only 10 percent are political in nature, that works out to 3,000 associations. I am aware of none in China—which doesn't mean there aren't any, just that I'm not aware of them. I was told in 1985 that someone in a unit attached to the Central Committee once tried to form an opposition party. But people are for the most part gripped by a mood of helplessness. They are indignant over injustices that have occurred and concerned over the dangerous path China is taking, but they feel there is nothing they can do (a feeling shared by many party cadres).

So where is the hope I referred to? In China it is very easy to be a pessimist, and one needn't search far for reasons. But if one looks beneath the surface, one can see the enormous vitality of the nation, its unlimited potential, and realize that the Chinese people have reached an unprecedented state of maturity. Let me tell you why I think so.

First, the awakening of the Chinese people, signaled by the 1976 Tiananmen Incident, has developed along new lines over the past fourteen years. I believe that this protest, which was instrumental in the overthrow of the Gang of Four, was a signal that the Chinese people would no longer be at the beck and call of the authorities. They had decided to participate in the course of their own history. Millions of people with no organization behind them and no newspaper to call their own went out into the streets to demonstrate, and not just in Beijing but in Xi'an, Nanjing, and Chengdu as well. This was a significant turning point. Several years have passed since then, and the people are more mature now, no longer so servile. Overcoming passivity has not been easy for the Chinese people in general or in particular for the Han Chinese, the majority in which Confucianism has been deeply embedded. I hasten to add that, in addition to ideology, the economic reforms played a role in this; hundreds of millions of peasants who had been so dependent for so long were liberated. This also includes people living in urban areas, who belong to a particular work unit for life, according to the pleasure of their leaders. They can punish you, or your wife, your sons, even their wives. But that has begun to change, for the Chinese people now have some mobility: if things do not work out, they can quit, simply walk away.

Second, a middle class has begun to appear in China, and even though it is not very powerful, and not very wealthy, at least it exists. I refer to the industrial and commercial entrepreneurs, of whom there are now 12 million in rural and urban areas. This figure should not be underestimated just because these are family operations. It is no longer uncommon for people in China to be worth as much as 100,000 yuan; that may not sound like much when converted to U.S. dollars, and my own life savings are no more than 10,000. But when you add 50,000 heads of private enterprises to the 12 million individual entrepreneurs and their families, the scope increases dramatically, for they employ anywhere from a few dozen to several thousand workers, and their wealth can run into the millions. One of my friends contracted to run a coal mine, from which he earned about 3 million. These contracts, struck on an individual basis, propel a person into economic activities independent of cadres working for the state. Such people must be considered the new capitalists.

There are also vast numbers of rural entrepreneurs who fall

into the same category. It is worth noting the new relationship between these people and the local officials. In the past, people bowed to party secretaries and government officials, whom they considered their betters. Now in many towns and cities, party secretaries bow to the entrepreneurs, on whom they have become dependent: they ask for help when there is not enough money in the coffers to run the government or party organization, and if one of them has trouble getting by, he calls on an entrepreneur. China has entered a new historical era, in which money is more powerful than authority.

Third, I believe that changes are occurring in the status of the Communist Party and within the party itself. The party's ability to control society and its various organizations has never been as low as it is today. It is no secret that factions exist within the party, even though they do not manifest themselves in any organizational way. This is yet another factor that must be taken into consideration when analyzing China's political future.

The final point involves my observations of Chinese society over a period of many years. Within the rigid framework of our political system, even if there are no significant changes in the system itself, changes can nonetheless occur beneath the surface, clear and distinct changes. And the process continues, with a greater and greater chance that the changes will have lasting force. Take the People's Congress, for instance, which is justifiably viewed as a rubber-stamp body. The election process for representatives has little claim to democracy, and when members vote for heads of government, they just check the appropriate box. I have never heard of anyone's voicing opposition or abstaining. But distinct changes began to surface in 1988. I was told that representatives from provincial, municipal, and county levels vetoed certain names on a list of candidates for whom they were supposed to vote. There is a provision that if ten representatives nominate a candidate, that person becomes a candidate. The vetoing has happened in a number of provinces, cities, and counties. Officials of one county in Shanxi put forward a slate of candidates, only to have them all defeated.

We have an old saying in China: "Playing with the false but resulting in the genuine." The possibility of turning the false into the genuine does exist in China, so that even fake organizations and so-called democratic mechanisms might someday become real. This is happening in the People's Congress. Newspapers have recently reported that China's trade unions are clamoring for reform, emphasizing participation in government and their watchdog functions. Reports like these are not official announcements, nor do they originate from the powers that be; to the best of my knowledge, they stem from changes within the unions themselves. No longer content to be mere branches of the government, they are determined to serve the interests of the workers. To this end, they have formulated a series of demands: they want to participate in legislation and be consulted on political policy that involves the interests of workers. My sources in China have verified the accuracy of these reports. Surely this has come about only after earnest deliberations. Thus government-run trade unions are in the process of becoming popular labor unions. Even though the appearance of a union like Poland's Solidarity is not considered a strong possibility in China, there is a distinct possibility that government-run trade unions will in fact evolve into popular unions.

Even under the unified leadership of the Communist Party and within a single system with specific policies, various locales, work units, and departments are not all run the same. They have drastically different degrees of freedom, from considerable to extremely limited. The *China Youth Daily,* where I worked for a while in the 1950s, is a case in point. In 1987, when the height of the campaign against bourgeois liberalization was reached, this newspaper took increasingly greater liberties, eventually becoming one of the most objective newspapers in China, second only to Shanghai's *World Economic Herald.* In 1988 its more than two hundred reporters and editors were so united that not one of them informed on anyone else. Many of the stories written by these reporters are fine examples of courageous journalism. During meetings of the People's Congress in 1988, for instance, the *China Youth Daily* published the speeches of Ding Shisun, the president of Beijing University, and of the noted economist Qian Jiaju, both of which were well received at the Congress. This upset the authorities, who took the newspaper to task. I assumed that the paper would be chastened by this criticism, but they leaped right back into the fray after some perfunctory self-criticism. This is a case of a government-run newspaper evolving into a popular one. There are other instances too. In 1987 the *Shenzhen Youth Daily* was closed down. I viewed this paper as an independent entity in 1986; even though the words "Published by the Shenzhen Communist Youth Organization" were displayed under the masthead, a few young people ran the newspaper in their own way.

To sum up, I sense that popular freedom is growing imperceptibly, that something is causing it to ferment. So even though the nation operates under a certain system with certain policies, a bold individual who can unite a group of people around him will be effective in running a county, or a newspaper, or a publishing house.

It appears likely that China will continue to develop along the uneven lines I have described, with one or maybe four provinces and seven or maybe a dozen counties leading the way toward political reform. Within the bounds of the charter of the Chinese Communist Party and the constitution of the People's Republic of China, they can go far, and the Central Committee will be unable to stop them. And with changes in the structure itself, I believe that the pace will be quickened.

THE FATE OF
INTELLECTUALS

It would be difficult to find another country like China where, in this century, intellectuals have played such a vital role in the fate of the nation and the progress of society. If we use twenty years as the standard for a generation, then there have been four generations of intellectuals since the May Fourth Movement of 1919, each of which has made significant contributions. Invariably it has been they who have aroused China's masses and propelled China forward. But each time, they have fallen short of their objective, leading in many cases to disappointment, dashed hopes, even utter dejection. And yet every ten years or so the Chinese people face yet another crisis, and these same intellectuals rise to the occasion.

We must first define the term "intellectual," which has a brief history in the Chinese language. At the beginning of the twentieth century, it was associated with the concept of "schooled and reasonable" and applied to anyone who had reached a certain educational level. As the level of education changed under the nationalist government during the war years, "intellectual" was used by peasants and soldiers to refer to anyone who had been to school; by the 1950s it had come to refer to anyone who had attended college. In recent years the term has signified scholars, professors, artists, writers, journalists, and the like, people whose professions involve independent mental activity. For my purposes, I will stick to the traditional interpretation of anyone who has received advanced schooling or achieved a comparatively high cultural level, including undergraduate and graduate students still in school.

Mao Zedong valued the historical significance of the May Fourth Movement and the role of intellectuals. The Chinese Communist Party is fond of referring to itself as the spiritual descendant of the May Fourth Movement. That was perhaps true during the party's early history, but applied to the period after 1949, when the party came into national power, it is a mockery.

Part of the May Fourth agenda had been carried out by 1949, including a triumph over imperialism and the establishment of China as an independent nation. But the struggle against feudalism was abandoned; although the feudal economic base was dismantled, the struggle on other fronts was terminated. In the 1950s, as China set out on its quest for wealth and power, the May Fourth tradition was discontinued, the nascent democracy movement was halted, and China began to move backward. In 1989 we celebrated the seventieth anniversary of the May Fourth Movement and the fortieth anniversary of the establishment of the People's Republic of China, as well as the tenth anniversary of the implementation of economic reforms. Coincidentally, these three celebrations occurred at a time when China was facing its greatest political and economic crises.

In the midst of the economic crisis that began to manifest itself in 1988, two social cliques, or classes, became prominent in the public eye. One is the bureaucracy, or bureaucratic stratum, which has enjoyed uninterrupted and unprecedented growth in the name of the proletariat over the past thirty years. This stratum was at first adamantly opposed to the economic reforms initiated in 1979, although it subsequently managed to milk these reforms to its own advantage, bringing the reforms to ruin. The leading clique, with Deng Xiaoping at its head, has used every weapon in its arsenal to bring the bureaucracy under control and minimize the harm it can inflict. But by all appearances the various directives of the Central Committee of the Communist Party have had little effect. For every policy at the top, there is a counterpolicy at the bottom. The other social clique in the public eye is the intellectuals, who historically have formed China's progressive nucleus; the current period of reform has provided no exception. But in the past ten years, living conditions for intellectuals have hardly improved at all, and recent inflation has threatened their very existence. Their contributions to society have been every bit as significant as those of their foreign, particularly western, counterparts and in many respects greater. Yet they earn one fiftieth, or one one hundredth or even one two hundredths, as much as intellectuals in the west. A friend of mine, who returned to China from the United States with a doctorate, earns as much in a month as he could earn in a single hour teaching abroad. The monthly salary of a university research or teaching assistant in Beijing or Shanghai is slightly more than 70 yuan (RMB), which is not enough for one person to live on. So the universities must supplement their income from research funds, and even then the increase is only 20 or 30 yuan a month, hardly enough to boost them above the poverty level.

Deng Xiaoping recently stated that the way to recognize the importance of intellectuals is to increase their salaries and to improve their situation; but even if the leading clique of the Communist Party were to make this a hard and fast policy, given the nation's empty treasury I doubt that money could be found for raises. But the core of the intellectuals' problems is neither the financial rewards they receive nor the degree of respect given them. Whenever the Communist Party examines its policy toward intellectuals, the invariable conclusion is that the party cadres underestimate the worth of the intellectuals. This is only the tip of the iceberg. When we look at the history of the Chinese Communist Party, it becomes obvious that it has always been anti-intellectual and has tended to view intellectuals as the enemy. Almost none of the intellectuals among the first generation of Chinese Communists (including the party's founders) has avoided coming to grief. The majority of party leaders who stood on the reviewing stand at Tiananmen Square during the founding ceremony of the People's Republic of China in 1949 were either high-ranking military officers or peasant leaders, even though most of the founders of the party twenty-eight years earlier had been intellectuals. This is highly significant.

In 1951 Mao Zedong initiated an event whose significance was as great as the campaign to suppress counterrevolutionaries: "the ideological remolding of intellectuals." The triumph of

1949 had brought people to the Chinese Communist Party in a state of euphoria; the intellectuals alone, particularly the most learned among them and scholars, writers, and academics with significant political influence, had the courage and knowledge to challenge the party's authority. In this campaign, Mao demanded that all intellectuals should make a clean breast of their historical, ideological, and moral errors and defects, compelling them to degrade themselves in front of the masses as a means of stripping away their prestige. For those renowned intellectuals who had lived and worked in Guomindang areas, the year 1949–50 marked their first experience of life under the rule of the Chinese Communist Party; their previous opposition to the Guomindang had earned them the reputation of progressive intellectuals, but they were not yet prepared to place their complete trust in the Communists. By 1951, the majority had been brought, more or less, into the fold.

Many members of this generation of intellectuals, born around the turn of the century, had participated in the May Fourth Movement; with the exception of natural scientists, after 1949 they accomplished nothing more for the rest of their lives. Creative writers are the most notable example: such first-rate novelists and essayists as Mao Dun, Ba Jin, and Bing Xin have written hardly anything over the past forty years. Lao She was virtually the only productive writer in their ranks, but with the exception of his play *Teahouse,* nothing he wrote during this period could compare in quality with what he did before 1949.

Shen Congwen was the smart one: following two unsuccessful suicide attempts at the height of the campaign in 1951, he abandoned his writing career altogether and took up research on the history of Chinese attire, thereby avoiding considerable anguish and reaping a degree of scholarly rewards in the process.

Among this generation of intellectuals, only the philosopher Liang Shuming displayed the indomitable spirit of "unyielding character" so typical of intellectuals in China's tradition. He had the courage to engage Mao Zedong in open debate, holding back nothing in his criticism of Mao's ultimate authority, and he stood up to the public attacks and abuse that followed. All the others either kept silent or, like Guo Moruo, sang paeans even to the blatant mistakes of the Chinese Communist Party, shamelessly selling their souls for all to see.

Between 1949 and 1966, sixteen nationwide campaigns were mounted, eight of which singled out intellectuals as the objects of criticism and attack. With the exception of the campaign against Yu Pingbo's "Research on *The Dream of the Red Chamber*" and the attacks on Hu Shi, the campaigns were protracted political struggles, and even though the targets were not labeled enemies, they suffered irreversible losses: they and their families could no longer stand tall. As for the remaining eight campaigns—including the 1955 campaign to eliminate counter-revolutionaries; the 1951–52 campaign against the three evils (corruption, waste, and bureaucracy within the party, government, army, and mass organizations); the 1952 campaign against the five evils (bribery, tax evasion, theft of state property, cheating on government contracts, and stealing of economic information)—intellectuals were not exempt from involvement.

Although each campaign had a particular focus, individuals unfortunate enough to become targets of any campaign were invariably exposed to general criticism. Charges included political views inconsistent with the Communist Party; unorthodox academic views (that is, diverging from the body of thought approved by officials of the Central Committee); moral conduct that did not meet proletarian standards; a lack of enthusiasm for work or for following the directions of party organizations; lacking the spirit of self-sacrifice; egoism; uncooperative behavior; a fanciful lifestyle; problems in relations between the sexes (romantic relationships not leading to marriage, divorce, and intimacy between unmarried persons were all subject to criticism); personal behavior or interests that varied from the norm (such as enjoying western music or using makeup). The central issue was inevitably "bourgeois individualism." Many of the charges listed above are subsumed under bourgeois mentality, while individualism (which in China is synonymous with egoism) is considered the root of all evils. The desires to develop one's talents, to be an achiever, or to become expert at something (even the desire of a writer to produce a classic work of art) are viewed as manifestations of the despised individualism. The wish for people to work toward an objective is considered a form of loyalty toward the party and the communist cause; but loyalty to the party is paramount. Absolute obedience and a spirit of selflessness in furtherance of the party's mission (normally understood as following the orders of the party secretary at one's work unit), with no doubts or objections, is expected. Criticism and investigations almost always involve family background and personal history. If your father was a landlord, a rich peasant, a capitalist, or an official in the old order, your personal problems are usually linked with this class background. If you received a foreign education, had "social contact" with high-ranking nonproletarian individuals or foreigners, were ever involved with nonparty organizations, or worked for organizations not close to the party, even greater weight would be assigned to mistakes or crimes committed after 1949.

The foremost sign of a desire to draw close to the Communist Party is the willingness to confess your past mistakes and mercilessly to criticize your current ideology and political attitude. You must also expose the problems of others in the same spirit. Intellectuals were quickly divided into the three categories of leftist, centrist, and rightist, based on their degree of obedience to the Communist Party. Being labeled a leftist worked to intellectuals' advantage in politics and in the workplace, for they enjoyed the privilege of membership at all levels of the People's Political Consultative Congress and the prestige of representation in the People's Congress or other social posts, thus enhancing the stature of their families.

It is difficult for most people to imagine the intensity of the political atmosphere of China in the 1950s. It was a result not only of epochal changes that had recently occurred and were spreading into all areas of life, but also of several political campaigns that were sweeping the nation: resist United States aggression and aid Korea, suppress counterrevolutionaries, remold the ideology of intellectuals, foster loyalty and honesty within party organizations and government agencies, and ferret out Trotskyites. People of all ages were diligently studying Communist Party ideology and policies in order to view life in a different light and adopt new attitudes. Politics thus became the prevailing force in everyday life. In such an atmosphere, intellectuals were hard pressed to muster the courage to maintain their individual personalities and views running counter to those of the Communist Party. At the same time, many professors and scholars, sympathizers and opponents of the party alike, were in awe of the brilliant accomplishments of the military and the political dominance of the party, some taking extreme measures in hopes of gaining membership.

China's intellectuals were far more compliant in their dealings with the Communist Party than those of the Soviet Union and Eastern Europe. In the twenty years following the 1917 revolution, some Soviet writers and literary theorists continued to contribute valuable work to the world. But nothing similar occurred in China. Even as late as the 1980s, Chinese writers had yet to match the courage of Hungarian writers of the 1950s or Czech writers of the 1960s. In 1956, intellectuals in Budapest initiated a movement to oppose Stalinist tyranny, which was squelched only by Soviet tanks. Less than a year later, China's intellectuals were caught up in a wave of constructive criticism of the Communist Party that resulted in a crushing defeat: a million people were labeled antiparty rightists. This discrepancy is naturally linked to differences in attitudes toward the Communist Party between the peoples of Eastern Europe and those of China, but we cannot disregard certain traditional weaknesses among China's intellectuals.

Some people find it difficult to comprehend how an intellectual like Guo Moruo, with all his talent and learning, could adopt such a slavish attitude toward the Communist Party and Mao Zedong. Most of the leaders of democratic parties who were engaged in a courageous struggle with the reactionary forces of the Guomindang obediently mouthed the party line after 1957. Even some former rightists willingly turned into conservative defenders of the party during the period 1957–1979. In a sense, these people were reliving the experiences of their May Fourth predecessors. In Lu Xun's stories, the "madman," who resisted the feudal tradition of cannibalism, goes "elsewhere to take up an official post" after coming to his senses; another character, Lu Weifu, who had sought to "remake China," calmly returns to his teaching of Mencius and the Canon for Girls; and the character Wei Lianshu is "now doing what [he] formerly detested and opposed, giving up all [he] formerly believed in and upheld." Lu Xun's brother, Zhou

Zuoren, who had once led the fight for "human liberation" and "free spirit," turned into a hermit in search of benign moderation. During the Japanese invasion, he collaborated with the enemy.

The appeal of name, position, and material benefits is so strong among some intellectuals that it can overcome the desire for truth and lead to a willing sacrifice of individual talent. Another advantage of "selling out" has evolved since 1949: the avoidance of being labeled a traitor or turncoat; the mantle of "the people" the Communist Party has wrapped around itself has consistently withstood all attempts to remove it.

Tragically, even the intellectuals' virtues have worked against them. Throughout China's history there has been a tradition among intellectuals to be concerned about country and people, and to "assume responsibility for governance," encapsulated in such sayings as "Be the first to worry [about one's country], be the last to enjoy" and "If the fate of my country demands my life, I will not refuse because of personal pain or self-interest." These have been mottos for generations, a self-sacrificing spirit that motivated many Chinese intellectuals to set out on the path of revolution in response to unimaginable events, either as founders or as ordinary members of the Chinese Communist Party; when they suffered injustices and persecution in their political lives, this same spirit made it possible for them to endure for the sake of the people or for the larger interests of the party. Since 1949, this trait has made it possible for the party to persecute and control intellectuals. To illustrate, during the anti-rightist campaign of 1957, the vast majority of intellectuals labeled as rightists knew full well that they had been unjustly accused. Yet only a fraction rose up in opposition; many, in fact, refused to bear a grudge against Mao Zedong for their having been the victims of such severe persecution, nor did they gain a clearer understanding of errors committed by the party. Instead, they acted according to the traditional teaching: "Suffer the indignities and bear the burdens." They forgave the party and viewed their own sacrifice as part of the inevitable price to be paid for China's progress.

Concurrent with this, intellectuals on the China mainland have become employees of a highly centralized state, leading to the loss of their political and economic independence and under-mining their independent thought. Over the past thirty-five years or so, intellectuals have lost the freedom to choose the nature of their work, as well as the location, the organization, and the conditions under which that work is undertaken; their salary, position, housing, freedom for spouses to work in the same locale, awards and honors, the opportunity to go abroad or per-form domestic assignments involving travel, are all determined by others. This sort of dependency relationship, by definition, makes it incumbent upon intellectuals to be subservient to party cadres that have the power to determine their fate. The loss of a sense of equality saps the courage to struggle.

But the true determination of the fate of intellectuals over the past forty years has been anti-intellectualism by the Chinese Communist Party and Mao Zedong. The antirightist campaign of 1957 was a natural result of this. Mao's 1942 "Talks at the Yan'an Forum on Literature and the Arts" has been the most influential and insidious of all his works. One cannot truly comprehend the pernicious effect this article had on Chinese history by reading it out of context. The key is to read it in the light of the history of the past few decades, for it establishes a theoretical framework for the role of intellectuals in the revolution under the leadership of the Chinese Communist Party: they must be dependent upon and obedient to the workers and peasants, whom they serve while cleansing themselves of the "original sin" of bourgeois individualism and remolding their ideology. They must sing the praises of society under the leadership of the party and never expose its dark side. The effect of the essay was to crush, once and for all, the intellectuals' critical spirit and rebelliousness. This philosophy has enjoyed uninterrupted development since 1949, forcing intellectuals to move through society "with their tails between their legs"; according to Mao, they are "strands of hair on the skin" of society, totally dependent upon others. "Wherever intellectuals gather, problems arise" and "The greater the intelligence, the deeper the roots of reaction" comprise the common wisdom. The 1957 antirightist campaign was a crushing blow to more than a million intellectuals; from that time on, China's intellectuals were reduced to a submissive existence, which has led to a whole era of silence.

Intellectuals were able to build an atomic bomb, but were denied any influence on the course of China's history.

Since May Fourth, we have seen four generations of intellectuals—"four generations under one roof." Most of the May Fourth intellectuals are gone, including Liang Shuming, Ye Shengtao, and Zhu Guangqian, all of whom died in 1987. Post–May Fourth intellectuals, who became active in the 1920s, were more numerous than their predecessors; but precious few of them have been able to express their opinions since 1979. I can count only three: Ba Jin, Xia Yan, and Xie Bing Xin. Only the remaining two generations have had notable effects on Chinese society; one is composed of people like me, now in their fifties or sixties. Middle-aged and somewhat older intellectuals have withstood the heaviest attacks and been saddled with the heaviest responsibilities over the past thirty or forty years, while living under miserable conditions. This generation has also been more deeply influenced by traditional Chinese culture. It can be interpreted as either the remote tradition of more than five thousand years or the nearer tradition of the past forty years; it also has two facets, positive or negative. The power of tradition evidently has some influence on this important generation, whose members are charged with China's heaviest responsibilities as university presidents and professors, editors, influential writers and theorists, even cadres at all levels of government, from the municipal to the Central Committee.

It is not farfetched to say that the majority of people at this level are supporters of the current reforms in China. But few of them have the courage to subject themselves to further political dangers. Those involved in ideological work, including philosophers, social scientists, and social critics, are a little better off than novelists and other writers. Friends of mine who are about my age are doing their utmost to pass on the newest thinking and information possible within limits allowed by current political realities. Some of them came under attack in 1978 and 1979 for advocating a thorough exposure and criticism of Mao Zedong's mistakes. I can list at least ten: the philosophers Guo Luoji of Nanjing University and Wang Ruoshui of *People's Daily,* the social theorists Li Hongling, Su Shaozhi, and Zhang Xianyang of the Institute of Marxism-Leninism, the jurist and publisher Yu Haocheng, the writer Wang Ruowang, the editors Ge Yang and Qin Benli, and the social theorist Ruan Ming. Each of these persons firmly supported free thought and opposed "whateverism" (from the slogan advanced after Mao's death: "Whatever policy suggested by Chairman Mao, we will support it; whatever Chairman Mao's directives, we will inexorably follow them"). Yet they all fell from grace, and the "whateverists" remain in power. Many intellectuals at this level have come to terms with the current order, becoming powerful supporters and benefiting from official appointments and high position.

Even more important is the generation born in the 1940s and

1950s, which reached adulthood during the early stages of the Cultural Revolution; they were less deeply influenced by the ideology of Mao and escaped the persecution inflicted on intellectuals of the 1950s. Why mention the 1950s? Because it was this persecution that made it impossible for intellectuals to hold their heads high, a situation that has not changed. This younger generation matured in the midst of the upheavals, destruction, and chaos of the Cultural Revolution. The first three years of the Cultural Revolution were a crash course for them, during which they experienced as much as my generation had in twenty years. They learned about Chinese society not from textbooks but from personal experience. Under the authority of Mao's slogan "Rebellion is justified," they vehemently attacked every aspect of Chinese tradition, ultimately attacking even Mao himself. They were fanatics during the early stages of the Cultural Revolution, enjoying a freedom my generation could never have imagined: they were free to attack whomever they pleased, to say whatever they pleased, to put up big-character posters, to publish magazines, even to shoot people if they wanted to. But it did not take long for them to become targets of the same abuse they had been handing out to others, and the persecutors became the persecuted. Having been forced to "go up to the mountains and down to the countryside" for as long as ten years, they not only observed but experienced first hand the dark side of the Communist Party and of society, as well as the suffering of the Chinese people.

In the early 1970s, when Lin Biao fell, the majority of this younger generation began to undergo a political awakening (the most progressive among them had started even earlier). They formed secret organizations to study theory, to examine China's problems, even to propagate what they considered to be the correct ideology among the masses. Many of these organizations were uncovered and their members executed for the crime of studying true Marxism. Even greater numbers were arrested for being members of counterrevolutionary organizations and sentenced to prison terms. It was this generation that formed the backbone of the Tiananmen Incident of 1976, and it was they who protested at the Democracy Wall in 1978–79. These young people had a keener sense of awakening and greater courage than my generation, and they were more thorough. In May 1977, five months after the fall of the Gang of Four, more than fifty young people who had been arrested under that regime, but not yet liquidated, were summarily executed by the Hua Guofeng–Wang Dongxing clique. Why were some people set free while others were executed? Simply because the latter went beyond opposition of the Gang of Four by opposing Mao Zedong as well, the unpardonable sin. I consider some of these people to be among the most revolutionary individuals known in China, including Wang Shenyou, a college graduate in mathematics from Shanghai Normal University. It is no exaggeration to say that the thoroughness of his criticism of Mao was second to none and came out earlier than that of any professional theorist or philosopher. But the death of only one of these more than fifty individuals, a worker from Changchun named Shi Yunfeng who escaped the attention of the higher-ups, was ever reported. None of the others ever made the newspapers or received posthumous redress.

The massacre of 1977 did not daunt the young people who followed, nor did the arrest of political criminals and dissenters like Wei Jingsheng in 1979. In early 1980, after the Democracy Wall political magazines had been suppressed and several political organizations disbanded, a group of young people in Guangdong formed the National Association of Independent Magazines. I received a copy of their manifesto. In the summer of the same year, during elections for university representatives to the District People's Congress, these young people boldly announced their dissatisfaction with the current regime. Interestingly, solely because they criticized shortcomings within the Communist Party in their campaign speeches, people like Xu Bangtai of Shanghai, who were elected as representatives to the People's Congress, were expelled from the party. Chosen by the people as representatives, they were deemed ineligible for party membership. And we are aware of Hu Ping of Beijing University, who for the same reason received no work assignment for years after graduation.

Many people in China feel that this generation of young people, who grew to maturity during the turmoil of the Cultural Revolution, is one of China's great assets. But they are disliked by China's elderly, who dismiss them as rebels, even accusing some of them of being remnants of the Gang of Four, for which they deserve punishment. I don't say this is true of all the elderly, just those who were forced out of office during the Cultural Revolution, who lost their power and were humiliated; this is all they remember of the Cultural Revolution, not that it was an event of their own making, the inevitable consequence of their leadership. So when Ba Jin proposed the building of a Cultural Revolution museum, they were enraged. They want to negate the Cultural Revolution, but not *that* particular Cultural Revolution. The generation of young people to which I refer is comprised of students who entered college in the years 1977–1979 and, upon graduation, joined the ranks of Chinese society. Some of them now work in private industry and commerce, others are in the publishing business, while others run non-governmental social-science organizations. Many are viewed with disfavor in official circles, but once they achieve a certain position or have accumulated a certain degree of wealth, they are grudgingly accepted.

Let me illustrate. One of these individuals was the mainstay of a political organization that came into being during the Democracy Wall incident. The disbanding of the organization taught him that in China political involvement requires a strong economic base. So he returned to his hometown, where he became an industrialist specializing in soft drinks. Now, several years later, he is the business magnate of his province, well respected by senior provincial officials. I am acquainted with five or six others who, in a period of three years, have introduced many aspects of progressive western thought by translating (personally or by commission) two hundred books, with four hundred more soon to come off the presses. This shows how much a few individuals can accomplish.

Yet the demands on China's intellectuals in light of the current transformation of Chinese society show that their level of understanding and organizational skills remain deficient. Over the past few decades, China's intellectuals have been little more than employees of the government, and there are few other countries where this state of affairs exists. Every intellectual faces the powerful Chinese Communist Party in isolation. Back in the May Fourth period, China's college students, workers, and businessmen had their own organizations, all of which underwent rapid development in the wake of May Fourth. In Shanghai, neighborhood federations were established, which were in marked contrast to the neighborhood committees of more recent years, for they looked after the interests of every family in the neighborhood, regardless of occupation, and represented that neighborhood at the municipal level. But these organizations ceased to exist after 1949, being replaced by unions, women's federations, and the like, all of which were arms of the Communist Party. The Chinese people no longer had their own organizations. This severely reduced the options for intellectuals: facing the powerful Communist Party alone, they could either meekly embrace the party line or simply remove themselves from the scene, becoming totally apolitical.

Today's Communist Party has changed—it barely resembles the prestigious party of old. The Chinese people have changed too. But the aspirations of intellectuals to function independently in accord with their own inclinations have not revived and remain in a deep freeze. A palpable fear of the power they confront has not yet dissipated; admittedly, there is reason to be wary of this power, which continues to monitor people's activities at will and is always prepared to suppress those activities. Vigilance by the Chinese Communist Party is also justified, for although most members of the younger generation engage only in legal activities, there are some who are fully prepared to adopt violent means to achieve desired ends. This situation grows more widespread all the time.

There are other problems with China's intellectuals that form obstacles to their progress: decades of living in hardship have created a strong sense of self-preservation, a fear of doing the wrong thing, and an increased suspicion of others, which manifests itself in dealings marked by overreaching cleverness and a penchant for scheming and intrigue. The effect of China's traditional moral values decreases with the age of the individual, eventually disappearing altogether. This is a cause for concern, for it can only lead to the increasing appearance of traitors in political life; many people have been sacrificed in the cause of selling out one's friends for personal gain.

No matter how one says it, the draconian methods adopted by
Mao Zedong and his followers to control and persecute intellectuals from 1949 to 1979—gathering public opinion in support of
the Chinese Communist Party—has pitted intellectuals against
the workers and peasants, who have rushed to the side of Mao in
every campaign. But that has now ended. The truth is that Mao
Zedong did not actually seek out their views; in 1957, for
example, at the beginning of the antirightist campaign, the title
of the second editorial to appear was "The Working Class
Speaks Out." Yet, to my knowledge, the workers knew nothing
about what was going on at the time. I was aware of the situation, and I knew that many workers and factories in Shanghai
were on strike in a show of opposition against bureaucratism
within the Communist Party. Yet when the powerful forces of
oppression rolled over us, large numbers of rightists like me,
who had refused to acknowledge our crimes at the time, gradually began to doubt that everyone around us could be wrong. We
must have committed some kind of error, so we retreated, step
by step, eventually acknowledging our errors by signing the
accusations. What a frightful power that is, truly frightful!

But then something phenomenal happened: there was a
reversal in the nature of this mainstay. Since my first speech and
first printed article in 1979, I have been subjected to several
attacks. Why then did I disregard the advice of some people to
back down? Why did I continue to write up to the end of 1986?
Because I could sense the forces behind me growing stronger

every day. In contrast to my position in the 1950s, I am secure in the knowledge that I have strong support. No matter how powerful the officials in front of me are, they will never be able to overcome the strength behind me. Events of 1987, including expulsion from the party, only served to prove the accuracy of my prediction.

When we examine China's problems, we must never forget that the Chinese people have changed after ten years of economic reform. There are still some old men who refuse to acknowledge these changes or who cannot even see that changes have occurred. It is possible that chaos lies ahead, perhaps even great upheavals. Yet I believe that China's intellectuals are aware of these changes, that they will take courage from them, acknowledging their own worth and dignity, and will boldly enter the unfinished struggle begun by Chinese intellectuals seventy years ago.

THE
BUREAUCRATIC
PARADISE

The word *bureaucracy* has two meanings in English: a governmental system and the people working within it. My concern is with the second meaning.

In 1989, when the citizenry celebrated the fortieth anniversary of the founding of the People's Republic of China, they discovered standing before them a vast bureaucracy, one that bears little resemblance to the revolutionary band of forty years ago. Many members of the Communist Party, including officials, have also discovered that today's Communist Party is a vastly different political force from what it was in 1949. Today they must sense with regret that China's people have lost the power to change the leadership of China's bureaucracy and that party members have lost the power to make changes in party leadership. They must realize just how many of the Communist Party's views and slogans were empty, that the slogans they hear today run exactly counter to the essence and practical implementation of the most heralded slogans of an earlier time. The word "people," for example, is used everywhere: the nation is called the People's Republic, the courts are people's courts, the police are the people's police, even magazine titles are adorned with the word—*People's Literature, People's Music,* and so on.

But where are China's "people"? They have grown less and less significant over the past forty years, more and more powerless; it has almost reached the point where they see themselves in the position of having to "submit to the will of Heaven." The mass line, Mao Zedong's creation, has been widely heralded, but the masses have never participated in the formulation of any major policy decision. In fact, political power in China has been an arbitrary, autocratic prerogative for forty years. And if we think back, for thirty of those forty years, we have been caught up in an increasingly violent atmosphere of class struggle, Mao's class struggle, the real targets of which ceased to exist in the mid-1950s, replaced by one or more invented enemies. Since class struggle requires targets, we continue to deal with China's landlord class more than three decades after Mao's own admission, three years after the land-reform movement, that the "decapped" landlords should no longer be regarded as landlords.

None of this should surprise us, since the last four decades of Chinese history have been little more than a history of the alienation of the Chinese Communist Party from its ideals. Many Americans and other westerners are of the opinion that the failure of Mao's experiment is a failed experiment of socialism and Marxism, thus constituting the essential failure of socialism and Marxism themselves. But Mao actually failed because his policies contravened the tenets of socialism and were in direct opposition to Marx's fundamental socialist policies. Marx never advocated socialism without freedom or a socialism that runs counter to concepts of humanism. Instead Mao placed the people in a subordinate, passive role as soon as the new nation was founded, reserving the dominant role for the party and the bureaucracy. For forty years Mao admonished the people to sacrifice their todays for a brighter tomorrow, to sacrifice their human values and freedom in the name of economic construction. As a result, all the todays have been sacrificed, and that tomorrow is farther away than ever; the people have offered up their freedom, sometimes their very lives, but economic construction is in shambles. If Mao had implemented one tenth of the precepts of the Paris Commune, there would not be such an enormous, impotent, and corrupt bureaucracy in China today.

Not only does China's bureaucracy, made up of Communist Party officials, differ from its counterparts in other countries, but it bears little resemblance to China's traditional bureaucracy. The standards for choosing cadres are unique. They first appeared among followers of the Red Army and the People's Liberation Army as they occupied new areas. The first order of business for the military was to gain an understanding of the situation in the new area and determine who were its potential enemies; to do this it was necessary to reorganize the people's lives and issue new government decrees. Inasmuch as officials of the previous regime were not to be trusted, activists willing to work for the new regime came to the assistance of the military and the party, and the most loyal and competent among them were recommended or appointed by military or party officials as local officials. The Chinese Communist Party disbanded the well-organized official system of the Ming and Qing dynasties, and also paid no attention to contemporary governing systems in other countries, decided against elections, examinations, terms of office, and supervision and systems of punishment. Disregarding history and the modern experience of foreign countries, the Chinese party established a system of control over a nation of nearly a billion people based upon its experiences in military control, in which a given area might be abandoned at any time. It is not a complex system: political fealty to the party is the prime consideration in appointing an official, far more important than abilities or cultural level; the reinstatement, promotion, or demotion of an individual is invariably determined by how an official higher up feels about him, rather than by his character, morals, abilities, or achievements, or by how the masses feel about him. The primary concern of an official is to carry out the orders of his superiors and, regardless of rank, to carry out the orders of the Central Committee; no consideration is given to whether the results will benefit or harm the local populace or people throughout the country.

Ever since the founding of the nation, or even earlier, during the civil war, there has been a tendency among Chinese officials to resort to coercion or, stated differently, lean to the left rather than to the right. This is something Mao Zedong knew very well, and he punished many cadres for it, but still he regarded it as a means to get things done, a work ethic. In China, the word "left" has unique implications above and beyond those it carries in other countries: it implies merciless and ruthless treatment of others. One ruthlessly attacks others in the class struggle and mercilessly exploits people's labor in production and construction, taking all their blood, sweat, and tears.

I recall an incident in 1952, when the Central Committee circulated an announcement regarding disciplinary action against a county party secretary in Shandong province. In retaliation against the local peasants, who had disobeyed his orders about seeding (linked perhaps to an order from the provincial committee), he ordered them to pull up all the green shoots and to reseed the fields with another crop. The stern wording of the circular is an indication of Mao's anger over the incident. But neither he nor the Central Committee utilized it to stipulate official policy and create a mechanism to prevent a recurrence of such incidents. Instead, they demanded strict obedience, discipline, and absolute loyalty to party organizations. Later in that decade, in 1958, the Communist Party intensified the requirement that cadres bend to the will of the party. This led to further alienation among party members, who were now to be mere tools.

This unique position of the Chinese bureaucracy has created a special temperament among its members. Since these officials have become docile tools of the party, and since their fate lies in the hands of their superiors, they maintain fealty only to these superiors, which in the long run forces them to implement policies and measures that are unreasonable, that violate their consciences, that are sometimes even inhumane. Over time their emotions grow numb; their senses of justice and of right and wrong gradually wither away. I have used the phrase "moral and political emasculation" to describe this phenomenon. Another reason for the symptom is that once a person becomes an official, he knows he is assured a good life so long as he commits no major mistake. The lifestyles and living conditions of these people differ greatly from those of ordinary citizens; they have their own troubles and their own joys. As a result, many of China's bureaucrats display attitudes of indifference: unlike most people, who sympathize with suffering and grow indignant over injustice, they no longer seem to experience normal human emotions.

A further characteristic of Chinese bureaucrats is their utilitarianism. "Political repercussions" is a popular term in the Communist Party lexicon; it means that one cannot seek a result without considering its effects in the political arena. In actuality, political repercussions have been virtually ignored by everyone from Mao down to the lowest cadre, whose primary concern has always been whether a particular course of action will bring quick success and instant benefits to the individual or to his faction. Only the objective is considered, never the means or the effects. This characteristic of the bureaucracy is reflected in China's economic construction, wherein the greatest effort of the Chinese people produces the least rewards. Over the past forty years, a trillion yuan have been invested in Chinese industry, of which only two thirds is currently in operation; the other third produces no benefits whatsoever. And the functioning two thirds operates at low efficiency with high expenditures. Chinese economists call this "hollow economics," which means unremitting expansion and inflation around a hollow core, with extremely slight benefits.

Then, too, these officials must sooner or later abandon independent thought, can no longer offer differing opinions, and must engage in lies and deception, even make false reports of achievements in order to please their superiors; they make empty promises and deceive the masses. Finally, once they reach a certain rung on the official ladder, the bureaucrats divorce themselves completely from China's realities, lost in a fantasy world or in memories of the glorious past. In their minds, the Chinese Communist Party maintains the high prestige it enjoyed in the 1950s, a mixture of authority and power over a populace that is obedient and gullible. To illustrate, during the 1980s I often heard high-ranking party officials complain, "The people hold up their bowls and eat fresh meat, then lay down their bowls and grumble." What they mean is, "Your lives are much better now, but you're still not satisfied and you blame the Communist Party. That is uncalled for." Still seeing themselves as benefactors, they feel that the people ought to be as grateful as they used to be in the early days—but those days are gone forever.

People who come out on top in internal party struggles, who not only survive but continue to climb the ladder, can be categorized as people who know how to trim their sails in any political wind, who seize opportunities to benefit themselves, cater to their superiors, are ruthless with the people, engage in merciless struggles and extortion, and attack others with extreme cruelty. Their opposite numbers, humanists and true Marxists, find promotion or even survival in the Communist Party extremely difficult. This has led to a sort of antiobsolescence process, the exact opposite of the struggle for survival in nature; on China's political stage, the race goes not to the fittest, but to the least fit. Today there are two kinds of people who flourish in the Communist Party: the mediocre (those we would call political hacks) and the opportunists (those with wild political ambitions).

There is no reason to delve deeply into the issue of bureaucratic corruption and criminal activity. Suffice it to say that anyone in an occupation where something is required from someone else—and this is not limited to officials in charge of personnel, finances, or commodity affairs—deals in graft and bribery or any other means necessary to obtain economic benefits. Graduation diplomas, both real and fake, passports, identity cards, even proof of tubal ligation or vasectomy, are all for sale. The most serious crimes or unlawful activities against the state, such as the illegal harvesting of trees, seizing cultivated land, and exceeding family-planning limits, are all fair game for party cadres; if they can get away with it, there is nothing to keep ordinary citizens from confidently doing the same things.

Chinese society still does not function under the rule of law. Incidents of malfeasance by officials is rising at the rate of 40–50 percent a year, but few offenders come under criminal investigation, since large numbers of officials are restricted only by party or administrative discipline. There is, in addition, a self-preservation mechanism built into the bureaucracy. The Communist parties of China and the Soviet Union differ greatly. China has ancient feudal traditions that deeply affect interpersonal relations: bloodlines, family lines, and geographical origins have created a system of common interests that unites many members of the Communist Party, forming them into factions or parties within the party. Power struggles within the Communist Party and struggles among factions seldom occur over major political principles or theoretical differences, as is true in the Soviet Communist Party. It is fair to say that the majority of the power struggles in China arise over personal interests. The same is true at the middle and lower levels, where all sorts of networks have been established since the party first came into power. These officials pass their authority back and forth—not in the abstract, but as perquisites of authority or the opportunities authority provides, such as employment, promotion, party membership, transference of census registration from the countryside to the city, and so on. Back and forth it goes: I'll help you by providing an opportunity; you help me by providing some commodities. The bureaucrats' children often intermarry, establishing a blood relationship or what is called a kinship relationship. There are also relationships that go back in time, such as place of birth or schooldays, all of which lead to extremely tight networks.

Among the counties I have visited, such as Bin county in

Heilongjiang province, anywhere from a third to a half of the local cadres can be linked together, thereby forming a powerful clique. If one man commits a crime, the network is mobilized to form a protective cloak around him; it is very effective. Two incidents can serve to illustrate; both involve county officials at the highest level—bureau heads—and both involve graft. In the first case, when the official's superiors sent an investigative team, many people came forward as witnesses and gave eight hundred pieces of false evidence to prove it was not a case of graft. In the second case, more than two hundred people came forward to protect a corrupt official. It is relatively easy for a bureaucrat to find a supporter among his superiors, that is, a behind-the-scenes patron; as long as this is a powerful individual—if, say, a county party secretary has a prefectural party secretary in his corner—protection is assured.

I once went to Hunan province on assignment and heard a story about Cixi county. Many officials in the local party committee and government opposed the local party secretary, who was indeed a terrible person, up to his neck in graft and corruption; but they were powerless to dislodge him from his position, for he was protected by the prefectural party secretary. I know of more than one party secretary whose evil deeds were reported to Hu Yaobang himself. In each case, Hu issued a directive to punish the individual and assumed that his directive was carried out; but such people can be the target of three or four directives without ever being punished. The sole difference between the situation now and that under the Guomindang is that no institution in China has the power to control corruption within the Chinese Communist Party. The Communist Party of today still relies solely upon its ability to reform itself, and thus far it has demonstrated only the failure of that ability. In the 1950s, Mao dealt a death blow to both the legal and the journalistic systems by labeling many people rightists, which of course is one of the prime reasons the party remains lukewarm about establishing a legal system. I referred earlier to the final stages of Guomindang control, by which I mean the last days of its control on the China mainland. Back then, the monthly salary of a county head was 300 silver dollars, that of a county party (Guomindang) secretary was 45 silver dollars. This shows the difference between party and governmental authority. Back then, a county head was scrutinized by the political section of the Guomindang county branch, the county judiciary and senate, democratic parties, local newspapers, and Communist Party underground organizations. Now, however, these all fall under the sole jurisdiction of the county party secretary. Recently people have been discussing which was more corrupt, the Guomindang on the eve of its retreat or the current Communist Party.

China's bureaucracy has become its own objective, a force that has expanded without pause over the past forty years, becoming more and more parasitic all the time. This expansion has occurred in contravention to the will of Mao Zedong. It baffles me how it has grown so strong, in light of the series of campaigns initiated by Mao to streamline government. In 1983–84, Deng Xiaoping initiated yet another such campaign; it also failed. I am talking not only about an increase in numbers but also in the rate of promotions within organizations and the increasing power of the organizations themselves. There is a hierarchy among China's administrative organizations similar to that among people: there are organizations at the section, department, and bureau levels. Organizations from Beijing down to the local districts have been upgraded, and some have been subdivided into two or more organizations. The publishing industry provides a good example: the Sichuan Publishing House was originally a single, efficiently run unit, but it has been divided into six or seven separate houses; similar situations exist in other provinces. What purpose does this serve? Where there was originally one director, there are now six or seven, and each house has its own leadership team, with room for even more unnecessary positions to be filled by even more people.

According to material released in 1989 by the Xinhua News Agency, where there was one department when the bureaucracy was established, there are now several bureaus or as many as a dozen departments. In one county in Jilin province, there was a total of twenty organizations under the auspices of the party committee and county government when party control was established in 1948, with 322 personnel. The population of the county, which was 130,000 in 1948, grew to 150,000 by 1955, while the number of official organizations increased to 32, employing 479 people. The number of organizations has now mushroomed to 150, employing over 2,000 people. How much does it cost to support all these organizations every year? In 1987 the county department of finance expended 4.1 million yuan for administrative costs alone, one tenth of the total revenues for that year. But this figure represents only a small fraction of the actual costs to society. There were 95 vehicles belonging to county, rural, and township governmental and party organizations, for which depreciation, maintenance, fuel, and salaries and bonuses for drivers totaled 2.56 million yuan. Annual expenses for food and beverages for officials (not all of which were reported) totaled 1.1 million yuan; the annual cost of building houses averaged 2 million yuan. These expenditures consumed more than one fourth of the county's total annual revenues and did not include the various perquisites enjoyed by officials.

Based on figures revealed by Mao Zedong in a 1957 speech, there were at the time 1.8 million officials throughout China. There are now 27 million. This figure may seem inflated, but according to a reporter who made a survey of five provinces in 1987, the ratio of nonproducing employees to workers in factories is often one out of three, sometimes even one out of two. In Luoyang's Yarn-Dyed Fabric Mill No. 1 (in Henan province), one factory worker supports eight employees. Admittedly this is an extreme case, but not an isolated one. In Inner Mongolia, for example, in the administrative area of the Xilinguole steppe, there are nearly as many cadres and their subordinates in the party and the government as there are herdsmen. In a certain northwestern nomadic county with a total population of less than 9,000 there are more than 800 party and government officials who are "chiefs" of something.

There are, in my view, two reasons for this state of affairs. First, since the Communist Party came to power it has, in contravention of the Marxist theory of a gradual withering away of the state following the establishment of authority by the working class, handed more and more social responsibilities over to the party and government instead of to the people. A look at the growing ranks of officials shows that the people have become an increasingly passive component in society and could not conceivably become the masters of the country. Second, prior to 1979, working for the government as an official was the only path open to personal development without courting disaster; since then, this has become the path not only to safety and convenience but to profit as well.

The bureaucracy and its power have evolved as a result of the mistakes and perverse actions of the party; its growth has continued in spite of economic disasters and a downgrading of the role of the people. The initial disasters occurred in 1958, during the Great Leap Forward, and the famine of 1960. The peasants went hungry, since food was controlled by the cadres; in the villages, peasants were willing to give everything they owned for grain that was sold back to them, including the sexual favors of their wives and daughters. Documented instances of this occurred in the northeast, in Heilongjiang province. Owing to vast differences between the cities and the countryside as a result of the economic disasters, everyone wanted to move to the cities, where they could be assured of a fixed amount of rations for food; the authority to transfer peasant census registrations from villages to the cities became a special privilege of the cadres, from which they derived considerable profit. The Cultural Revolution, during which the Chinese people faced even greater hardships, gave rise to still more special privileges. Great numbers of young urbanites sent down to the countryside needed to return to the city to work, to continue their schooling, or simply to improve their lot by joining the party; to reach this goal, they paid tribute to cadres and bribed the leaders with gifts and, in the case of young women, their maidenhood. Victims of unjust accusations by the Communist Party, or their offspring, pleaded with bureaucrats, or gave them gifts and bribed them, to have their verdicts overturned.

An impoverished country like China is made even poorer by the cost of supporting the bureaucracy, particularly the upper echelons, who enjoy a standard of living that is sometimes higher than that of many officials in foreign governments. Their modest salaries are supplemented by perquisites equaling several times that amount. These people constantly receive valuable gifts from their hometowns, from places where they have worked, or from people or organizations for whom they have done favors. Since they receive more food than they can eat and more things than they can use, they trade off the excess to build up a surplus of good will and increase their network of connections. Meanwhile, they have established an international reputation of gross inefficiency and incompetence. Abandoning modern communications media, they prefer the more comfortable methods of agricultural villages, holding meeting after meeting to promote work. How many people are lodged in Beijing's official guest houses at any given time to attend meetings in the capital? Forty to fifty thousand. A national meeting on the chemical industry was held in Shandong province in 1988, at which an incredible sixty thousand were in attendance. Railroad officials complained that there were not enough trains to handle the increased load.

Every corrupt practice in life in China is hidden from view. But in 1988 something finally occurred that could not be concealed: the value of RMB. All corrupt practices in Chinese society are reflected in the declining value of RMB. It is no exaggeration to say that devaluation of RMB and inflation were the underlying causes of China's current crises. "Bureauprof" became rampant, and profiteers raised havoc with the national economy by appropriating public funds to set up privately run companies; in 1988 over thirty companies were established, twenty-six of which were engaged in commerce. They used public funds to corner the market on scarce raw materials and essential commodities. This speculative profiteering led to an increase in the price of aluminum from slightly over 4,000 RMB a ton in March to 18–19,000 in September, resulting in the closing of 90 percent of the manufacturing plants using aluminum as raw material.

Chinese society entered a period of unrest and chaos in 1987; according to recent official reports, from 1985 to 1987 there were 7,000 incidents of armed resistance over grain and tax collection, resulting in more than ten deaths, over a hundred serious injuries, and many lesser injuries. Everyone knows that the Chinese are a patient, obedient people; for them to rise up like this signals a true crisis. But the Central Committee of the Chinese Communist Party, unlike those in the Soviet Union, Poland, or Hungary, is unwilling to initiate political reforms and lacks the will or the power to deal with bureaucratic corruption. The people are justifiably concerned. First, there are increased possibilities of a rebellion that could lead to a fascist dictatorship. Second, there are fears about the emergence of a new class of individuals, resembling the bureaucratic capitalist clique of Guomindang rule forty years ago.

The Chinese Communist Party believes that Chinese history entered a new age in 1949, signaling the end of a bureaucratic class once and for all; there would be no more "official" ranks. In fact, there was a time when the word "official" no longer existed; officials were all known as "revolutionary cadres." But in less than a decade, contradictions between the bureaucracy and the people caused grumblings in the cities and the countryside, and within two decades even Mao himself was talking about a "bureaucratic class." Today this clique, or stratum, has become the least restrained and richest segment of China's population. Mainland China has become a bureaucratic paradise. The picture that has emerged is almost comical. On the one hand, the political representative of the bureaucracy, General Secretary Zhao Ziyang, announced in 1987 a "clean government" directive to stamp out corruption within the party and the government; on the other hand, in 1988 members of the bureaucratic stratum, high and low, who had a firm grasp on their special privileges, initiated an unprecedented plundering of the Chinese economy, arrogating billions in public assets to themselves. While the government worried about having sufficient funds to purchase farm products from the people, the profiteering bureaucracy, controlling tens of billions of RMB, engaged in illegal commerce. While the government sold fertilizer, diesel oil, and pesticides to the peasants at controlled prices, the bureaucrats withheld commodities to raise the price and reap staggering profits. Since the 1960s, the government has issued at least a hundred directives to limit the purchasing power of social groups, but the bureaucrats have rendered these directives useless.

The Beijing *Economic Daily* once reported: "A river of gold, formed of public health services, feasts and banquets, indiscriminately provided goods, expenses for meetings, travel expenses, automobile purchases . . . is flowing unchecked into a bottomless 'black hole.'" Commentators use the astrophysics term "black hole" when referring to China's expenditures for social groups, which suck up the nation's wealth without giving anything back. It is not a groundless accusation. Statistics issued by China's Bureau of Statistics show a rapid increase in expenditures for social groups: currently they exceed a hundred billion yuan annually, consuming nearly half of the national revenues. One foreign friend exclaimed emotionally, "China is a paradise for consumers of public funds!"

While a tenth of China's population remains underfed, 13.5 billion kilograms of high-quality food are thrown out by restaurants every year, enough to feed 34 million people for a year. The reason for this waste is that most banquets are paid for out of public funds. Everything the government has tried to restrict the use of public funds for banquets has proved fruitless. The results of a survey of nine factories in Shanghai showed that the average expenditure for "banquets" grew at the annual rate of 49.3 percent over a three-year period. The monthly banquet expenditure for entertaining officials at all levels of a certain clothing factory ate up 34 percent of its profits.

Today, as inflation causes nationwide panic, the importation of high-quality consumer goods continues to rise. During the first six months of 1989, more than 10,000 automobiles were imported, a 57.6 percent increase over the preceding year; the importation of cigarettes increased 67.1 percent, and the number of jeeps more than trebled. Where does the money come from? It is siphoned off from an already pitifully inadequate school budget, subsidies for the poor, and agricultural supports. Meanwhile, exorbitant taxes on the peasants have increased.

It is worth noting that at a time when China faces not only a worsening economic crisis but a growing crisis of trust by the people in the Communist Party, the bureaucratic stratum has launched an all-out attack against conventional means of seeking personal gain; adopting reckless methods, with no thought for the consequences, they seek to destroy the people's economy and personal lives in pursuit of even greater ill-gotten gains. For instance, under the instigation and acquiescence of local party committees, they use state-run enterprises to manufacture bogus liquor, cigarettes, and medicine, to increase the bulk of milk with dangerous additives, to manufacture fertilizers and pesticides that are not only ineffective but include ingredients that damage the soil and the crops, and to replace good seed with infertile varieties. Although these practices are strictly forbidden by the government, they increase several fold each year. Corrupt officials in Shaanxi borrow money from the state, then reinvest it at a high rate of interest; party and government officials in Hubei embezzle over a billion RMB from a bank (nearly one third of the bank's total funds) earmarked for the purchase of farm products in order to build private homes, give lavish banquets, buy the favors of women, and engage in illegal speculation.

All these activities are undertaken with the tacit approval of the senior leadership of the Chinese Communist Party. I am not implying that Chen Yun or Deng Xiaoping is in favor of such activities, but party leaders oppose reforms in the political system that would effectively curb and eliminate this powerful segment and its criminal activities, thereby giving free rein to the bureaucracy to continue its outrageous behavior.

In the process, however, the bureaucrats have begun to earn their just deserts: all this free-wheeling corruption has begun to enrage the Chinese nation, normally the most generous and easy-going of people, which can only hasten the demise of the bureaucratic dynasty.

FREEDOM OF
THE PRESS

China's economic reforms, in place now for over a decade, have indeed initiated enormous changes. Scholars, both Chinese and foreign, generally focus their attention on the program itself, which is proceeding methodically and systematically from the top down. What has received less attention is an even more important process going on at the same time. The people have received not only economic freedom but also, quite contrary to the wishes of the party leaders, a degree of individual independence. The peasants are no longer at the beck and call of local officials. For the first time in thirty years, they are their own masters. This has set in motion changes in lifestyle, in ways of thinking, in family relations, even in the relation between the sexes: all realms of activity are involved. Such transformations are more widespread, more thorough, and more profound than any occurring in the economy. By way of contrast, changes in the ideological control and direction of China's official circles do not match changes in the people's thinking. Evidence of change in the controlled newspapers, or more accurately in the news media, has been sparse in comparison with what we see in literature and the arts or in scholarly research.

In my estimation, among intellectuals in China, novelists and poets, that is, creative writers, enjoy the greatest freedom; reporters enjoy the least. To illustrate: China Central Television (CCTV) recently aired the documentary series "River Elegy," which was intended to reflect upon the negative influence of traditional culture on Chinese history but which actually criticized party conservatives and called for political reform. If this had been written into a novel or served as the subject of scholarly research, I doubt that it would have caused such an uproar among government authorities. But since it was shown on national TV, a component of the news media whose influence is of enormous concern to the Communist Party, Vice-President Wang Zhen himself publicly condemned the series, expecting *People's Daily* and CCTV to follow his lead. But, instead, General Secretary Zhao Ziyang came to its defense.

This incident underscores an important characteristic of China's social progress over the last decade: the declining influence and control of the party over society. The gap between the wishes of the national leadership, particularly the conservative faction, and its ability to carry out those wishes is growing daily. And even though control over the print media is somewhat greater, changes are still occurring.

Let me tell you how the newspaper business works in China, since few foreign friends are familiar with it. There is no organization explicitly charged with censoring the press. So where does the censorship come from? From the editors-in-chief, the directors of the various departments, and individual editors and reporters. Naturally there is a system of supervision: all newspapers on the national level, including *People's Daily,* the party's central organ, have members from the Politburo or party secretariat who are assigned supervisory responsibilities in addition to ideological supervision. In this system the party's Propaganda Department wields considerable authority. As a passing point, let me say that I have been to the Soviet Union on four occasions and never once learned the identity of the director of the Soviet Union's Propaganda Department. But in China the functions of the central Propaganda Department are far more critical than in the Soviet Union. The Propaganda Department and the Press (Mass Media) Bureau, which is under its auspices, directly supervise the newspapers, beginning with *People's Daily*. They employ what we might call "postpublication censorship": after an issue has been published, members of the Central Committee are free to criticize whatever contents they find objectionable, and the newspaper is forced to recant.

During my first three years with *People's Daily,* the newspaper received telephone calls just about every day from people trying to meddle in our work, including officials as senior as Hu Qiaomu and Deng Liqun; even their superiors, such as Chen Yun, frequently had their secretaries complain to *People's Daily.* Deputy heads of the Propaganda Department, bureau chiefs, even section chiefs, were also free to criticize the paper. That was during the years 1979–1982. *People's Daily* was able to ward off or ignore some of the criticism, but most of the time there was no option but to engage in self-criticism, even if the charges made no sense at all; we had to deal with them, whether we believed they were wrong or not. Usually, three or four months after the self-criticism, the newspaper could start publishing stories very much like the one that got it into trouble in the first place. But this was not the case until the late 1970s; in the 1950s or 1960s it would have been unthinkable. In theory reporters are free to cover any story, without restrictions. But in reality every reporter and editor, including editors-in-chief, do not need to be told which stories must be covered, which are off limits, and which fall into gray areas.

Some of the criticism involves delicate matters like printing something on the front page that should not have appeared or running an editorial that contains politically erroneous statements. This is serious. Lesser problems include complaints from senior officials whose names have been omitted from coverage of meetings and conferences, or whose photographs have been placed on page three instead of page one. The decision on whether a reporter's story will be used generally lies with the head of one of the editorial departments. Major stories, or potentially controversial ones, are approved or killed by the editor-in-chief or his deputy. High-ranking officials sometimes direct that stories they consider important be published, and editors are forced to comply, even if they feel the story is inappropriate or suspiciously motivated.

China's newspapers enjoy a peculiar degree of freedom, which generally undergoes one or more changes every year as a result of changes in the nationwide political atmosphere, moving between degrees of relaxation and tightening. *People's Daily* enjoyed rather more freedom between the years 1978 and 1980, and we were relatively bold. Admittedly, this was due in part to certain needs of the Deng Xiaoping clique, specifically the need for criticism of the Cultural Revolution and of leftist forces. At the time, Deng's economic reforms were encountering powerful obstacles. His rural policy of household farm output quotas, for instance, was blocked by certain provincial party committees for four straight years. *People's Daily* played a major role in promoting economic reforms and other significant measures at the time, such as redressing grievances of unjust accusations and removing rightist labels. Nowhere in the decisions of the Central Committee or in any of its directives dealing with rightist rehabilitation could you find statements that all rightists were to be rehabilitated; only a fraction qualified, on a case-by-case basis—if you were unjustly charged you would be rehabilitated.

My own case is telling. I was labeled a rightist on direct orders from Mao Zedong, which meant that I entertained no hope to be included in the ranks of the rehabilitated. After reading the directives, I believed that even if only 10 percent of the total were denied rehabilitation, I would be included in that number. During the latter part of 1978, *People's Daily* published a series of important articles, one on the front page, which stated that sixty-three former cadres of the National Security Ministry labeled as rightists in 1957 were all to be rehabilitated, with no exceptions. This brief announcement sent shock waves from one end of the country to the other, where officials were watching. How many people are going to be rehabilitated?

they wondered. Now that *People's Daily* had run this story, they knew that the Central Committee intended to rehabilitate almost all of the rightists. Ultimately, with four or five notable exceptions, such as Zhang Bojun and Luo Longji, all rightists had their verdicts overturned.

The degree of boldness at *People's Daily* is the presence or absence of support by a politically important individual. Hu Yaobang was a behind-the-scenes supporter of *People's Daily* for a long time. During the 1981 Bai Hua incident, for example, although newspapers of the People's Liberation Army published one critical article after another, *People's Daily* remained on the sidelines, without publishing a single criticism of Bai Hua. My paper was able to avoid participation, despite the involvement of the PLA, because the campaign was not led by Deng. Everyone at *People's Daily* knew this, and we knew that Hu went from ambivalence to opposition where this campaign was concerned. But as his influence weakened, the degree of freedom enjoyed by *People's Daily* also decreased. In short, every editor and every reporter know exactly where newspapers stand in China, and they have a clear sense of the size of the playing field. They can contend only within the field of play, whose size expands and shrinks in accordance with changes in the political situation. Within prescribed limits, reporters and editors, especially editors-in-chief, can take certain initiatives and, if they are bold enough, enlarge the playing field somewhat. Even in bad times they can expand the degree of freedom.

As a consequence, a contradictory state of affairs has existed in China in recent years. On one hand, the Central Committee has been systematically reducing the degree of freedom of the press, step by step, leading to the situation in 1985, when I was not allowed to publish anything. On the other hand, peculiar though it seems, that same period witnessed the appearance of newspapers that took considerable liberties, such as the *Shenzhen Youth Daily* and Shanghai's *World Economic Herald*. Early in 1987, during the campaign against bourgeois liberalization, the *Shenzhen Youth Daily* was closed, but the *World Economic Herald* was protected. Interestingly, Beijing's *China Youth Daily* became an extremely liberal newspaper just at that time, which confirms what I said earlier, that centralized control is gradually being eroded as the Chinese people exert greater and greater pressure on the party. In response to the power of an awakened populace, some reporters, myself included, have shown a willingness to write stories that displease the Central Committee, even in the face of mounting pressure, manifested in fierce attacks and strong opposition.

Like a human face, official organs of the Chinese Communist Party reveal the party's standing, the relationship between it and the people, and its own true nature. To illustrate, newspapers have withheld reports on issues of vital concern to the people's lives for thirty years (throughout a period of increasing material hardships), reports on social problems of greatest concern to the people (crime, accidents, disasters, questions of morality), preferring to preach in stern tones; the people listened to the preaching in the 1950s and 1960s, but as time passed, readers wearied of the interminable sermons. Critical stories and exposés, favorites of the people, are often killed by meddling high-level cadres, while obituaries of bureaucrats and revolutionary memoirs of officials, which the readers detest, fill the pages.

People expressed serious doubts over this kind of party organ in 1956–57, but every one of them was labeled a rightist (the ratio of rightists among journalists is higher than in any other group, exceeding 10 percent and reaching 30 percent or more among editors and reporters on some newspapers), with the result that after more than three decades of publication, the party organ has no idea what a newspaper is supposed to be.

A major controversy arose several years ago after a speech by Hu Jiwei, the head of *People's Daily,* in which he said that newspapers ought to belong first to the people and second to the party, that their first responsibility was as the voice of the people and only then as the voice of the party. This was in 1982. The party's chief ideologue, Hu Qiaomu, attacked Hu, keeping it up for several years, until just recently. In his view, a party organ must first and foremost be the voice of the party; when we talk of the party's standpoint and the people's standpoint, the party's always comes first. In Hu's contrary view, the party had committed a number of errors over the years; based upon that experience, a party organ must not be the handmaiden of the party, so that when the party is wrong, the newspaper should resist or reduce the harm inflicted by those errors.

The Chinese Communist Party attaches such importance to *People's Daily* that it demands that every sentence and every word represent the will of the party and be absolutely correct. The party confidently assumes that every editorial and story has the power to cause waves and vibrations throughout society; that anyone criticized in its pages turns into a social pariah, while those who are praised immediately become august personages. They do not seem to understand that these ancient agenda produce the opposite results.

In fact, the debate over whether the party newspaper ought to be free to criticize party cadres and organizations actually began over three decades ago. I was personally involved in two major struggles over this question. When I think back now to the 1950s, I realize that some of the senior leaders of the Chinese Communist Party opposed freedom of the press as a matter of principle, believing that the official organ of the party should not enjoy the freedoms of the western press, since it was after all the party's newspaper. At the time, everything the west had to offer, including democratic systems, was seen as bourgeois, and the sentiment was that the proletariat should create a new form of freedom, that is, proletarian freedom and democracy. This is how they thought at the time: if the newspapers were allowed to print critical stories or exposés, that would damage the prestige of the party and threaten its interests. Second, the masses would be thrown into confusion at a time when it was necessary for the people and the party to share a common ideology; there was a fear that disunity would arise between the people and the party. Third, they were worried that such criticisms would become weapons in the hands of China's enemies, the imperialists. But from the late 1970s on, when I returned to the world of journalism, I began to realize that control of the press was no longer a matter of principle among the opposition, but that they were merely protecting their own interests, that criticism and exposés were a threat not only to their personal interests but to their very survival.

The stated reasons for opposing the publication of critical stories normally took one of two forms: first, the criticisms were branded as false; second, the critics were accused of destroying stability and unity. Allow me to return to the issue of the voice of the party. During the antibourgeois campaign in 1987, a movement, filtering down from the Central Committee to every province and municipality, was initiated to overturn verdicts of people who had been criticized by me and other reporters; in no time at all, criminals and people who had committed serious errors were suddenly heard from, as they accused us of spreading false criticisms and engaging in a campaign of liberalization. They demanded that our verdicts be overturned, and the front pages of newspapers were filled with the demands. So if we look at newspapers from 1987, we must ask: If the newspapers are the voice of the party, to whom are we referring? In large measure, the so-called newspapers have become the voice of a select group of privileged members of the inner circle. The people who attacked us were the very ones whose graft we had previously exposed.

China's party newspapers have committed a number of crimes over the decades. For every error committed by the Communist Party, its official organs have been willing accomplices. The graver the error, such as the 1958 Great Leap Forward and the 1966 Cultural Revolution, the greater the degree of complicity in demagoguery and deception by the newspapers. This lesson has never been subjected to serious scrutiny. Fabrications of "high production" in 1958, for example, were concocted on a daily basis and published. In this respect the military even went so far as to reward the reporter in its ranks who made the highest claims of accomplishment, whether true or not.

The restriction of the flow of news over a long period of time has resulted in an ignorance of important news by the Chinese people. Unaware of the true circumstances surrounding many major events in China, they were mentally unprepared for the galloping inflation that struck China in 1988 and wondered why prices suddenly skyrocketed. This led to widespread pessimism and panic. One of the strangest phenomena of the past forty years has been that the Chinese people learn about major events in their own country only through foreigners. When China's leaders meet foreign dignitaries (including overseas Chinese), they frequently divulge incidents that have occurred in China or plans for major events in the future; these visitors then inform Chinese-language broadcast media overseas, which transmit the news back to China. News of the December 1986 demonstrations that began in Hefei at the University of Science and Technology of China, then spread throughout the nation, was leaked to foreign journalists by their Chinese counterparts, and this major news story was then transmitted back to China via the Voice of America.

What China needs most now is an independent, freely run newspaper. The party may have had reasons in the early 1950s to suppress all nongovernmental newspapers and allow only party newspapers to operate, but that reason no longer exists. The people came to have complete faith in the party and placed their fate in its hands. But history has proved that the Communist Party has committed a number of errors and that it continues to commit them today. During the Great Leap Forward and the People's Communes, newspapers played a major role in furthering these mistakes by fabricating false reports of high production; this helped to cause the Great Famine. The Central Committee has never subjected this series of mistakes by the newspapers to serious scrutiny, nor, for that matter, the even more odious role they played during the Cultural Revolution. The people's mistrust in the newspapers has now reached serious proportions. In 1979 the circulation of *People's Daily* was over seven million; it has now dropped to three million, a major portion of which is paid for with public funds. The people's disgust with the newspapers was reflected in the demonstrations of 1986–87, when students at Beijing University publicly burned copies of the *Beijing Daily* on campus. Some students even used copies of the newspaper to wipe themselves and then mailed them off to the party secretary of the Beijing municipal committee.

Allow me to touch upon the role of foreign correspondents in China. News of the fall of the Gang of Four was first announced by a British News Agency dispatch. The Voice of America (VOA) broke the story of the 1986 student demonstrations. The freedom enjoyed by foreign correspondents in Beijing exceeds that of Chinese correspondents in Moscow in the 1950s. In China you will find them everywhere that foreigners are allowed to travel. They must exercise caution and take certain precautions to avoid giving the impression that they are hostile to the Chinese government. And they are not always free to report what they choose. The VOA has tens of millions of listeners in China, but it is very cautious, lest the Chinese government accuse it of stirring up trouble among the masses. In 1987, with the party expulsions I was involved in, the VOA audience no doubt increased many times. But the VOA sometimes disappoints with its excess caution, as with Hu Yaobang's fall from power, when the announcement nearly duplicated the official Chinese announcement, with no commentary.

The appearance of the *Shenzhen Youth Daily,* an official publication that evolved into an independent newspaper in the Shen-

zhen Special Economic Zone, and the increasing liberties taken
by newspapers throughout the country since then have inspired
optimism where prospects for the newspaper industry are concerned. But there are worrisome signs as well. As recently as
March 1989, a member of the standing committee of the Political Department of the Central Committee said that journalistic
reforms are necessary, but that neither the system nor journalistic concepts would be changed. So where are the changes to
occur? Larger headlines? Livelier layout? More photographs?
Changes like these have been made for years, but what about
improvements in substance? Chen Yun attributes the growth of
Poland's Solidarity to liberal trends among the country's newspapers. A glance at today's newspapers in China shows that the
Central Committee does not intend to expand freedom of the
press. They have entrusted specialists with the responsibility of
formulating laws governing the news industry, and in the past
few years, three or four draft propositions show that there is
some interest in improving the situation. But none of the pro-
posals has yet to be approved. Interestingly, even the term "freedom of the press" is unacceptable, so while literary freedoms
can be tolerated, journalistic freedoms cannot. Intellectuals are
concerned that laws governing the news industry will impose
new restrictions on the press rather than ensure safeguards. This
is in marked contrast to the situation in the Soviet Union where,
as a result of glasnost since 1985, a number of newspapers have
begun to enjoy considerable freedom. No newspaper or peri-

odical in China enjoys freedoms comparable to *Moscow News, Literary News,* or *Spark.*

Reporters also occupy a low rung on China's social ladder. Since 1987 reporters have been arrested on three occasions, after which they were beaten or locked up and deprived of their freedom. To this day we have never heard of any official coming to the defense of China's maligned newspapermen. Two years ago, for the first time since 1949, a reporter was tried and convicted for slander. It has happened twice more since then. Certain members of the Central Committee, aware of their precarious position, have grown particularly sensitive to reports from the international community, fearing chain reactions within China. The South Korean government's acceptance of eight demands by opposition parties last year is a case in point. Only two of the demands were reported in China's newspapers: one was for the direct election of the president, which was a nonissue for China, since the office does not exist. The demands they did not dare publish included the release of political prisoners and expanded freedom of speech. If these had appeared in print, the people might have had the idea that if such things could happen in South Korea, they could happen here too.

So far as I know, not a single underground newspaper or periodical exists in China. There are plenty of print shops in the country, with all the necessary equipment; business is so slow that many of them have had to close down, placing their employees, who get no more bonuses, in financial straits. But these shops are tightly controlled, and everything they print must first be approved by certain offices, with letters of introduction required from party or government departments. Even photocopy machines were controlled last year; copying shops, public and private, required signatures from everyone who wanted to copy something, and a list of the documents to be copied.

In sum, the lot of workers in the newspaper industry is a difficult one. Some of its finest representatives, not content to remain silent, have come up with ways to publish stories they believe the public deserves to see. Not allowed to express their views directly, they are often forced to employ circuitous means to get them across. In 1982, even though I was forbidden from attacking party corruption in *People's Daily,* I could not resign myself to the situation. In the spring of that year I went on assignment to a city in Jiangsu province, where I employed a roundabout means of writing my story. I began with a few lines praising the county and municipal committees for taking charge of party trends, then turned to the real business of writing an exposé, and ended the piece by returning to the struggle by party committees to solve their problems. Sometimes it is also possible to publish something the party leadership would find offensive by writing a misleading headline. For example, *People's Daily* recently ran several articles on the proposal for construction of the Sanxia Reservoir, a hot topic of discussion throughout the country. Many scholars and lay people in China

oppose the project, fearing that it could lead to disastrous consequences, but Deng Xiaoping and Li Peng avidly support it,
wanting desperately to complete work before they (Deng in particular) leave the scene. There were no indications in the headlines that the reporters opposed the project—they appeared, in
fact, to be supportive. But when you read the ostensibly objective stories carefully, it becomes obvious in the way they
reported the views of various people, pro and con, that the
writers opposed the project.

It is becoming increasingly apparent that the primary forces
capable of promoting freedom of the press in China are the
worsening national crises and the people's disaffection with the
current state of affairs; they are propelling China onto the road
of progress. In recent days there has been an increase in negative
news stories and exposés of the bureaucratic profiteers. This is
not because someone on the Central Committee is advocating
such stories; instead it is the inevitable consequence of rampant
corruption in Chinese society and the plight of the common
people, a means of defusing the people's anger. Rather than
being resolved, these crises are growing more serious by the
day. That is why I believe that in the not-too-distant future,
increasing pressure by the people will result in the creation of an
independent press. Early in 1988 the Public Opinion Institute
of Beijing University polled two hundred high-level individuals
(58 percent of whom were members and alternates of the People's
Congress, vice-chairmen and other members of the People's

Political Consultative Conference, members of the Central Committee and the Central Advisory Commission, and leaders of democratic factions, none below the rank of bureau and department heads and their deputies). Some 75 percent of the respondents felt that China's news media are not free to criticize or oversee the work of senior officials in the party and government; 92.5 percent felt that major political, economic, and social events should be reported. More than 80 percent felt that open debate in the newspapers on basic national policies and important issues involving politics, economics, foreign affairs, and social problems should be permitted. And 34 percent said they were in favor of having a daily independent (nonparty socialist) newspaper with national distribution run by a nonparty socialist organization. Whether or not these views will someday be translated into reality depends in large measure on the efforts of China's newspapermen. Sadly, Mao Zedong's line, which has determined journalistic policy for so many years, has reduced the number of outspoken and competent reporters to a pitifully small minority. But, I am glad to say, there are many recent graduates with bachelor's or master's degrees joining the ranks of journalists. One sixth of *People's Daily* consists of these bright young people. They are more courageous than the older generation, and more creative. Hope for the future of China's journalism rests in them.

WHY THERE
IS HOPE
FOR CHINA

How could there not be hope for a major country like China? But this is a real issue, for since 1985 many Chinese have begun to have doubts and it is becoming a hotter and hotter topic of conversation. There is a fire raging in the hearts of many people who are concerned with the state of China's affairs, burning as fiercely as the devastating forest fire in the Great Xing'an Mountains. We ponder anxiously: "China, O China, is there any hope for you at all?"

China is unquestionably beset with crises, with more and more dangers cropping up all the time. I have had this feeling too since 1985 and as a result have grown most troubled over China's fate. It is a natural and reasonable reaction.

Let us look at the facts. In the wake of economic reforms, China's gross national product per capita still lags far behind most of the rest of the world and continues to move backward. In 1979, China's GNP per capita ranked 108th in the world; by 1985, it had fallen to 126th. In 1979, China was on a par with Haiti and Pakistan, ahead of Sri Lanka and Sierra Leone; but now all four of those countries have moved ahead of China. The increase in GNP in many countries of Europe, North America, and Asia is several times, and in some cases over a hundred times, greater than China's. The United States's, for example, is 115.4 times greater. This disparity may be explained by differences in the two countries' histories and social conditions, but the same argument does not apply to some of the countries in Asia as compared to China. Beyond this, there is the destruction

103

of China's natural environment: two hectares of China's forest disappear every minute, and China's arable land has shrunk by half since 1949; the birth rate has far exceeded plans, with official statistics putting the population at 1.1 billion in 1989. China's natural resources are sufficient for a population of no more than 1.5 billion, and the current prediction is that within forty years, by the year 2030, China's population will reach that 1.5 billion figure.

Of course the greatest anxieties among the majority of China's people concern problems they face today. According to official statistics, China's rate of inflation in 1987 was 18 percent, and reliable documentation shows that the figure was actually more like 32 percent. Owing to energy shortages, many of China's factories operate only three to five days a week. Criminal activity is climbing at an annual rate of 30–40 percent. Economic reforms are nearly at a standstill, while political reforms will not be accomplished within the foreseeable future. This state of affairs has already begun to attract the concern of foreign friends. I received a letter recently from a Dutch sinologist, in which he said: "Recent news from China is terribly disturbing. It seems that no one holds out any more hope for the reforms, and what little sympathy remains is rapidly disappearing. From here it looks like China is in danger of entering a period of Brezhnevism, with decreasing production, a lack of confidence, and rampant corruption."

All three problems do indeed exist. But the current situation in China is vastly different from the Brezhnev era in the Soviet Union. First, the Soviet Communist Party of the 1960s was still in complete control of society, and the economic stagnation occurred in a climate of political order. But the Chinese Communist Party has already lost control of society and of the party itself, and China has entered a period of economic, political, and social chaos. Second, the Chinese people as a whole have not lost faith in the reforms; instead they are dissatisfied with the system. What they have lost is their faith in the Communist Party and the present political system, and this is not true in most of the Soviet Union. Even more important is the fact that the Soviet Union did not have an economy like China's twenty years ago, nor does it have one today; China's current economy includes a large-scale private sector and a highly developed entrepreneurial component. As recently as a few years ago, officials in the Chinese government either paid no attention to the private sector and the entrepreneurial component, or they viewed them as insignificant, unworthy of notice. But now they have emerged as factors that cannot be ignored. The private sector of the economy already accounts for 10 percent of all industrial production. And in commerce 20 percent of all retail sales in the country are generated by the private sector. The backbone of commerce and the service industry is the network of shops, big and small, of which China now has over 10 million. In Guangdong province alone, private savings exceed 36 billion yuan, most of it the savings of private industrialists and businessmen. These people and the entrepreneurs now possess the means to buy out small and medium-sized state-run enterprises, and not just in theory, for it has already happened. In Beijing and Guangdong a number of small state-run enterprises that operated at a loss have been bought out by individuals. People frequently worry that the Chinese government will change its economic policy and set into motion another campaign to eradicate capitalism. But I can say with conviction that this is not possible, because there are already 25.9 million people working in private industry and commerce, a labor burden the Chinese government is powerless to assume, even in the best of circumstances. Another strange and widespread phenomenon is that some state-run enterprises find it necessary to borrow money from private sources, since they do not have enough capital of their own. Even some local governments turn to these private enterprises for help in alleviating funding problems.

Among the many crises China faces, the crisis of spirit has become one of the arguments used to prove that no hope exists for the nation. The puzzlement, pessimism, and indignation felt by people all over China is a phenomenon very much worth examining, for it is unprecedented in recent Chinese history—never before have I seen this sort of despair. But I continue, nonetheless, to see hope for China.

In 1948, the year before the retreat of the Guomindang, people on the mainland lived extremely bitter lives, far worse than today; but back then there was no despair, no pessimism. Does that mean that the Chinese of the 1940s were better than those of today, that we have taken a step backward? I don't think so. In the 1960s, China experienced a catastrophic famine, in which more than 30 million people died. Yet even then the people expressed no dissatisfaction with the Communist Party. At least we didn't see any of that in Beijing, and I believe it was also true in general. Does that mean that the Chinese of the 1960s were more progressive than those of today? I don't think so. The mood of the people in the late 1940s was better because there was a perceptible political force on the scene, and they knew that the Communist Party would come to their rescue. And there was no indignation among the people in the early 1960s because they had strong faith in the party. But now they cannot perceive a political force that can solve China's crises, nor do they have any faith in the party. Viewed historically, this is, I believe, a good thing.

The people believe they are powerless to improve the state of affairs or to exert any influence; they are helpless, their hands are tied. The natural consequence of this sense of helplessness is that great numbers of people have sunk into despondence. But it can also be a call to action for other people to reform the system, for it is the current political system that has caused so many people to feel so helpless. During the six months I was at Harvard in 1988–89, there was a tremendous increase in actions by the Chinese people, from rational dissent to irrational violence; these have not just begun, they have already gone a great distance.

The three open letters sent by China's intellectuals to the standing committee of the People's Congress and the Central Committee of the party beginning in February constitute a major breakthrough in China's democracy movement, a true beginning. These letters broach the subject of human rights, which has always been taboo in China. The Chinese Communist Party has never allowed the people to mention human rights. Broaching this subject, or demanding the release of political prisoners, has always been the single most dangerous activity one could undertake. But I believe that the significance of this episode lies not in the fact that intellectuals broached the subject, but in the way they conducted themselves; this is the first time in forty years that they have openly challenged the Central Committee by putting forth a list of demands and pleading their case in front of the people and the world. What does this represent? It represents the last time they will come to the Chinese Communist Party as supplicants. After the first open letter was published, a spokesman for the Ministry of Justice made a public response, which was actually an attempt to squelch this sort of activity. The second open letter was not long in coming, and it brought out a spokesman for the State Council—that is, the next higher level—who took a harder line. The third open letter appeared shortly thereafter. This was a clear indication of the disregard in which the intellectuals were holding the nation's highest authorities. Why were they so bold this time, when they had never been so outspoken in the past? Among the petitioners were many scientists, artists, and writers of advanced age and high position who, for the past thirty or forty years, had been content to concentrate on their own scholarly and creative activities, never daring to express political views in opposition to the government. That was because for thirty of the past forty years, the workers and peasants, who comprise the main body of the citizenry, stood with the Chinese Communist Party, which enjoyed absolute superiority in the public mind. An episode like the intellectuals' open letters could occur only if the people of China no longer unconditionally supported the party.

More events of a similar nature occurred during this period. For instance, a group of representatives of the People's Congress, a total of at least two hundred intellectuals, writers, and scholars, spoke as one to oppose construction of the Sanxia Reservoir. This is a major project with a long history. After more than thirty years of discussion, the Chinese government recently decided to begin construction. Opposition from the intellectuals forced a concession from Vice-Premier Yao Yilin, a member of the Politburo of the Central Committee, that no construction would begin on the reservoir for at least five years. Then he abruptly executed an about-face, announcing at the People's

Congress through the director of the Hydroelectric Bureau that work would begin in two years. The announcement was met with opposition from representatives of the Congress and intellectuals, some of whom were themselves representatives, and in a very interesting, unprecedented manner. More than a hundred Chinese journalists, writers, and scholars published a book within fifteen days—no book had ever been published in China with such speed—and organized a press conference at which they announced their firm stand against the reservoir. All this appeared to produce results, for although everyone knew that the prime supporter of the project was Li Peng, the government has made no further mention of it.

Another struggle erupted around the issue of "new authoritarianism." Those of you who come from China know that new authoritarianism is a political concept formulated by certain intellectuals in conformity with the intentions of the leadership of the Chinese Communist Party. Its premise is that in a backward society like China's, where democratization is not viable, the model of Hong Kong, Taiwan, South Korea, and Singapore should be adopted, establishing a strong autocracy to get the economy on track, which would then gradually give way to a system of democracy. During the People's Congress convened in the spring of 1989, a great many articles opposing new authoritarianism appeared in party newspapers. While the congress was in session, more than two hundred intellectuals convened a separate gathering in Beijing to debate the issue, resulting in a tide of majority support for democracy.

All these activities by intellectuals occurred under the influence of support from the people. At the same time, the mood of the people influenced changes within the party. These are clear indications that liberal factions in the party may adopt the tactic of openly and collectively leaving the party as a means of expressing opposition. The so-called democratic parties have begun to get restless, and one of the leaders of a small party called the Zhigong, made up of returned overseas Chinese, recently announced that they would no longer accept funding from the Chinese government. Since these groups all depend upon the government for their financial existence, by refusing funding they are making it clear that they seek independence. At a recent congress of a larger party, the Democratic League, many of the representatives opposed the election of the Communist Party candidate, Fei Xiaotong, as chairman, advocating instead the election of the independent, critically minded economist Qian Jiaju. Qian, who is disliked by the Central Committee, was not chosen as chairman, but he was elected vice-chairman.

For some years now I have realized that I view the current situation and the country's prospects for the future differently from many of my friends. Prior to March 1988, before leaving for the United States, I made a point of asking every Chinese intellectual I met in Beijing: "Is there anything in your experience that could give us cause to be optimistic about China's future?" I got virtually nothing but negative answers, but I recall receiving a telephone call from the writer Zheng Yi in Shanxi, who told me he not only saw cause for hope but was optimistic about future prospects for life in general and for creative writing.

One characteristic that differentiates China from other countries is that many problems manifest themselves only in a circuitous manner. Making determinations about affairs in China based on surface appearances is a good way to be taken in. Since early 1987, for instance, college students have clearly grown dispirited, but that does not necessarily mean that they will never again be concerned with politics or that they no longer hold out any hope for success in the struggle for democracy or that they have lost interest. I was taken in once in 1980. Students from three universities—in Liaoning, Sichuan, and Fujian— came to my house for discussions in the summer of that year. They didn't come together, but what they told me was identical: they said that members of that year's freshman class were far less interested in politics than freshmen from the years 1977– 1979, and that was because they were entering college directly from high school and lacked the political experience of members of the classes ahead of them. I believed them. But then in 1985 I visited Nanjing University, Wuhan University, and several others, where I had quite a surprise. The students listening to my speech were more enthusiastic than those in 1979 and

1980 and asked far more questions. I concluded that, unless someone is successful at transforming China altogether, the Chinese people will not lose their interest in politics, for there will always be unresolved problems affecting their basic existence.

In my first essay I said that the path China follows from now on will differ greatly from the one taken by the Soviet Union. Allow me to sum up once again my views on the subject, this time with somewhat more precision.

First, I believe that future historical events in China will not be determined by the will of high-ranking members of the Communist Party, but will occur spontaneously among the Chinese people. We do not expect to see the emergence of a Gorbachev in China in the immediate future. Even if a man like Hu Yao-bang were to burst on the scene, I don't believe he could solve the problems we face today or extricate us from the dire straits we are in. I don't know why, but whenever observers comment on the state of affairs in China, they frequently overlook the main character in China's history—the people. This is the case with the party's Central Committee as well as supporters of democratic movements, both inside the country and overseas. Is that because the people show only their passivity and keep their active side hidden? In the final analysis, the fundamental cause of the fall of the Gang of Four in 1976 and the beginning of Deng Xiaoping's reforms was a resolute twenty-year work slow-down by the peasants, starting in 1958 when communes were established. Many saw only that the peasants did not rise up in active protest from 1959 to 1961, when China was suffering from a catastrophic man-made famine, or saw only that many peasants wept bitterly when news of the death of Mao Zedong reached them, overlooking the fact that the long and widespread work slowdown by these same peasants, old and young, male and female, who seemingly were so saddened by Mao's death, served to hasten the fall of Mao's dynasty. Now, from the mid-1980s on, it is China's workers who have fulfilled the historical mission of those peasants by their own increasingly intense work slowdown. In fact, an important and irreversible cause of China's current economic predicament is the workers' intentional reduction of labor efficiency and the increase in production spoilage as a protest against the current system. The people's anger and resentment will appear in even more discernible forms in the future. In a word, this is the foundation of all real change in China.

Second, China's political system will not undergo the kinds of changes we are seeing in Eastern Europe and the Soviet Union; there will be no multiple-party system and no truly democratic elections. Yet there will be more and more changes within China's political system, quiet internal changes that will escape notice by outsiders. At the same time, owing to public dissatisfaction with the increasingly reckless criminal activities of destructive elements within the party, the government, and the military, an intensified alienation and reduced production within work units, as well as a lack of cooperation with outside units, will lead to paralysis in certain departments, even disintegration.

My third point involves the increasingly important role in the political arena of progressive forces within the party, primarily intellectuals but also including some enlightened officials. At a time when the emergence of an opposition party is not possible, progressive forces can, to a certain degree, fill that role.

Fourth, the Communist Party's control over society and its own membership will continue to weaken, which will in turn strengthen the tendency toward local independence and autonomy. China is a large nation whose various regions are dissimilar in natural conditions, economics, and degree of political development; moreover, since the implementation of economic reforms, there has been an increased tendency toward local decentralization and self-support. After Deng Xiaoping passes from the scene, the prestige of the Central Committee will be further weakened, which will lead to conflicts between local regions and a weak Central Committee. It is possible that democratic forces will gain the upper hand in several provinces or in certain districts in some provinces, transforming them into a new form of politically "liberated areas," which will then expand outward. The newly created economic forces include managers of some state-run enterprises; when they merge forces with the intellectuals, they will comprise the main strength of progressive politics in China's future.

But China's progress will not be speedy. Economic reforms are at a standstill, and the possibility remains that there will be high-level reverses. The Chinese will pay a high price for the chaos that has already occurred and the chaos likely to come. But in the midst of the unavoidable suffering ahead, the Chinese people will throw off the burdens of thousands of years of history and tradition. That is, during the days ahead, the Chinese people will learn a new lesson, one that history has never before taught them: they will master the art of taking care of themselves and learn how to organize themselves in the cause of constructing a total democratic system. There are two possible scenarios: one is peaceful, rational action from bottom to top. In some counties and villages the people have organized themselves, spontaneously and independent of party leadership, to carry out tasks they believe are necessary. This is a comparatively calm and reasonable method. The other scenario involves violence.

There have already been many newspaper reports of violence. I will relate only one, in which some people chose a violent path when they realized that the government was either unable or unwilling to protect them. Not far from my hometown, in a small county called Hulan in the northern range of Heilongjiang province, a person who styled himself the Robin Hood of Hulan appeared on the scene (actually, it may have been one individual or a group of them). He (or they) announced a plan to get rid of one hundred policemen in Hulan county, eleven of whom had already been killed. The police in Hulan no longer dared to wear their uniforms on the street. When the people in a neighboring county learned what was happening, they put up a poster that said, "We welcome inspection tours in our county by the Robin Hood of Hulan." I know that similar incidents, eliminating lawless elements and protecting the good, killing the rich and relieving the poor, also occurred in Shanghai and Jiangxi in 1985.

My point is that reforms have a firm foothold in China, if not in the lives of every individual, certainly in the lives of the vast majority. They are now a fact of life, a mighty torrent that cannot be stemmed. There are Gorbachevs in many of China's towns and villages. Rumor has been making the rounds that there have been personnel changes in the upper ranks: specifically that, under pressure from the aging leadership of the Central Committee, it has already been decided that at the next meeting of the Central Committee and Military Affairs Commission, Zhao Ziyang will be stripped of his posts of party general secretary and first vice-secretary of the Military Affairs Commission. But over the past few years I have lost interest in such changes: as far as I'm concerned, no amount of administrative change, no matter who rises or falls, can stem the flood that is China's reforms.

In my speeches at several American universities throughout 1988, I urged my audiences to take note that China will become democratized through means that are uniquely different from those of the Soviet Union and Eastern Europe. During this century, from the Boxer Rebellion through two periods of Guomindang-Communist cooperation and two splits, through the Communist victory of 1949 and the Cultural Revolution, China has gone beyond all expectations on each of these occasions in the way it has made its history. The many crises currently facing China are at a critical point. As I speak, in 1988, it is clear to me that something will happen next year that will exceed everyone's expectations, and China will become the center of world attention. Pessimists underestimated the changes wrought in China by ten years of Cultural Revolution and over ten years of economic reform, and could not see the unprecedented reservoir of vitality among the Chinese people. Some may disagree with my views, but I will not abandon them. No matter how much trouble the enemies of the Chinese people cause, China's reforms will continue to advance, and in the process of reform, in the process of the struggle for political democratization, the people will transform themselves, giving rise to new changes in their beliefs and aspirations.

DENG'S
PYRRHIC
VICTORY

Deng Xiaoping regards the massacre at Tiananmen Square as a great victory. Hundreds of thousands of dissident students and their supporters were brought under control, and order was restored to the streets of Beijing. The truth, of course, is that the uprising was the greatest show of democratic force in over forty years of Communist rule. It gave the Chinese people confidence in their strength and exposed the deep rifts within the party leadership. The movement ended with the old ruling clique returning to the old political system, but its grip on the country is more feeble than ever. The extraordinary power of China's democracy movement is now clear.

When Hu Yaobang, the reform-minded party secretary, was ousted from office in 1987, the student movement on university campuses retreated. Many thought that the students, demoralized and temporarily defeated, had lost interest in politics and that there would be no more large-scale demonstrations. No one foresaw the events precipitated by Hu's death in 1989. On April 16 a small number of students gathered at Tiananmen Square to place wreaths in his honor. By April 22, some 200,000 students had defied a ban to carry out a demonstration of mourning, with over 100,000 onlookers expressing sympathy. Afterward, over 300,000 students petitioned the government through peaceful demonstrations; 3,000 of them went on hunger strikes, winning the support of over a million people, including intellectuals, workers, entrepreneurs, and ordinary citizens—an unprecedented event in Communist China. The students' political maturity could be seen in their organizational discipline and rationality.

In sharp contrast are the isolation, weakness, hypocrisy, and brutality of the Communist rulers. Two general party secretaries have been dismissed within two and a half years. And it was only by forcing every provincial party committee to declare its support for the dismissal of Zhao Ziyang and the appointment of Jiang Zemin that the top central leaders were able to gain the formal majority necessary to pass this measure. These leaders themselves are largely controlled by eight senile "retired emperors," all over eighty, who do not hold formal office in the party or government but who prop up their rule through brute force and lies. Deng and his cohorts have lost the confidence of the Chinese people and thus the legitimate right to rule.

Americans often ask whether the Chinese people's demands for democratic reform spring from the influence of western culture. It is true that during the reform era many books were published that discuss western society and political thought; that the return of foreign-educated students has spread democratic thinking in society; and that the Chinese people have been exposed to western culture through the mass media. But these influences alone never could have brought about such an enormous movement. Tiananmen Square was the inevitable result of a fundamental breakdown in China's internal political, economic, and social structure.

Since the beginning of the reform and open-door policies of 1978 and 1979, the Chinese economy has grown rapidly. The new agricultural system gave the peasants (who constitute 80 percent of the population) incentives to increase production; and the growth of local enterprises and the influx of foreign capital and technology prompted rapid industrial expansion. The flourishing of free markets brought about a rise in people's standard of living.

But economic growth was accompanied by an explosion of social and political problems. Deng Xiaoping not only repeatedly refused to carry out political reform; he tried to whittle down the few freedoms people did enjoy. Economic reform ran into all kinds of bureaucratic obstacles, and the party rectification campaign, aimed at stemming the tide of corruption and the degeneration of party ethics, ended in failure. Graft and embezzlement and other uses of public office for private gain became rampant at all levels of government. Serious crimes increased rapidly, and official profiteering ran wild. By 1983 the crisis was evident; by 1985 it had become pervasive.

The ouster of Hu Yaobang and the campaign against bourgeois liberalization in 1987 created more anger and despair, as did the soaring inflation. Chinese intellectuals, rooted in a tradition of serving the nation as a natural duty, adopted an attitude of silent protest against a series of party-orchestrated political campaigns. Then last February three groups of intellectuals signed open letters addressed to the authorities demanding human rights. Two months later university students—who are least bound by traditional thinking and have not lost their vigor and their sense of justice—resolutely marched from their campuses in mourning Hu's death.

One doesn't have to look far to discover how this crisis came about. Deng Xiaoping was attempting to promote economic reform while stubbornly insisting on upholding the Four Principles (the socialist path, the leadership of the Communist Party, the dictatorship of the proletariat, and Marxism-Leninism and Mao Zedong thought). His opposition to bourgeois liberalization and his desire to preserve Mao's overarching ideological and political framework were clearly at odds with his economic goals. It was inevitable either that economic reform would break through the old political order or that the old political order would act as a brake on economic reform.

Henry Kissinger, among others, likes to point out that it was Deng who initiated the idea of reform in the first place. *Time* magazine even selected him twice as Man of the Year. It is hard to reconcile the image of a leading advocate of reform with that of the executioner who crushed the democratic movement and then formed an alliance with those who had been the harshest critics of his policies. But Deng is a pragmatist, not a reformer. This is the man who in the 1960s noted that it doesn't matter whether the cat is white or black—if it catches mice, it's a good cat. After his return to power in 1978, faced with an economy devastated by the

Gang of Four, he resolved to dismantle the Maoist economic structure and to introduce practical reforms that would arouse people's enthusiasm for production. This did require courage and spunk. At the time the conservatives were very influential. Some provincial party committees simply refused to go along with the new policies; others adopted a wait-and-see attitude.

In Deng's efforts to cross old ideological boundaries, he urged Hu Yaobang (then chairman of the organization department of the Central Committee) to redress the cases of those falsely accused of political crimes during the Cultural Revolution, and to rehabilitate intellectuals who had been labeled as rightists during the antirightist campaign of 1957. These measures gained him widespread support. He subsequently encouraged Hu to initiate debate over the slogan "Practice is the sole criterion of truth," which was a guiding principle of the reform ideology and established a more solid theoretical justification for modifying the Maoist economic system.

The object of these actions was not to revamp the system radically, but simply to strengthen Chinese Communist Party rule, to prevent rebellion by those whose political consciousness had been raised during the Cultural Revolution, and to consolidate Deng's power within the party. The real test of his zeal for reform came with the Democracy Wall Movement in late 1978. At first Deng supported the wave of protest. But the next spring, when his position was more solid, he cracked down on the movement. At about that time he issued the slogan "Uphold the Four Principles, and oppose bourgeois liberalization," an indication that he meant to preserve Maoist ideology. He could tolerate and even encourage attempts to correct ideological mistakes in the party only as long as his political power was not fully consolidated. As soon as his position was secure, and his economic policies under way, he reverted to a conservative ideology and politics.

To Deng, as to Mao, people are nothing more than instruments: in wartime they serve as soldiers; in peacetime they are hands for production. The common belief of both leaders is "If I conquer the mountain, then it is I who sits on the mountain." ("I" is the party, which fought for power and thus has the legitimate right to it.) Only the leader can give orders, and the people must be docile and obedient.

People had gained a certain degree of economic freedom from the reform and open-door policies, but when they demanded democratic political rights, when hundreds of thousands of people shouted "Deng Xiaoping resign!" at Tiananmen Square, the leaders had the gall to say that "it is not only the case of a few individuals who cannot distinguish right from wrong, but we are dealing with the dregs of society and a gang of rebels who want to subvert our country and throw out our party."

Despite his supreme position, Deng of course did not act alone. Those who have significant influence include party elders Chen Yun and Bo Yibo, who have made every effort to derail economic reform; Hu Qiaomu and Deng Liqun, who stubbornly uphold Maoist ideology; Peng Zhen and Li Xiannian, who favor "old people's politics" and refuse to retire; and Wang Zhen and Yang Shangkun, who cling to a superstitious belief in military force. It was inevitable that Deng would be influenced by this faction. Having spent much of his life in the military, he too has an almost mystical confidence in the power of the military. With the help of these ossified ideologues, he destroyed the reform project that he created. They all refuse to see that the political system is destroying itself from within.

During the forty years since the party took over, twice it was forced to make concessions to the people, in 1960–1962 and in 1978–1980. Owing to the famine created by its own erroneous policies, the party had to give the peasants more economic freedom; there was also some relaxation of political control. But as soon as the 1959–1962 Great Famine was over, Mao took back the limited concessions he had made, both economic and political. It was the same with Deng Xiaoping. He had to grant the peasants economic freedom to boost agricultural production. In order to promote that program, he had to talk about political reform, but after 1980, he never mentioned it again.

Confident in his political supremacy gained by the Liberation, Mao was sure that the people would support him, no matter what material hardships they had to endure, including starvation. Deng also thought that since the people benefited from the economic reforms he advocated, they should not complain about the lack of political freedom. Three times Deng launched nationwide campaigns to oppose bourgeois liberalization and three times suppressed student demonstrations. His aim is clear: to maintain the old political system.

Misunderstanding on the two opposing sides had an influence on the 1989 democracy movement. The people still had illusions about Deng. In their view it was only the old hardliners who wanted to oust Hu Yaobang, and so they thought that Deng would not use military force to put down the movement. On Deng's side, he thought that, inasmuch as the people had tolerated the three campaigns against bourgeois liberalization, they would again cower under pressure from the government. He never suspected that the menacing threats of the April 26th editorial of *People's Daily* and the proclamation of martial law would not work to intimidate the people. Neither Deng nor the students had anticipated the decisive element in the 1989 protest: the participation of millions of Beijing citizens. Nor had they anticipated that so many officials from the party, the government, and the army would take to the streets in support of the students.

Deng was mortally shaken. Never since 1949 was there such an open split in the party, not to mention so many army officers who refused orders to suppress the students. Moreover, the mass media, ever instructed to be the voice of the party by the hardliners, also began to rebel. In about a week's time, in mid-May, the major newspapers and broadcasting stations in Beijing freed themselves from party restrictions and accurately covered the demonstrations. It was the first time since 1949 that journalists were able to defy regulations and act like true journalists. This period of press freedom, though brief, had a tremendous impact in promoting democracy movements in small and middle-sized cities across the nation.

But the long-time ideological restrictions the party exercised on the media greatly hindered the democracy movement. The overall situation of crisis in Chinese society and the development of the people's political awareness was barely known by the intellectuals, the students, or the citizenry. Almost everyone was pessimistic about China's future. No one was adequately prepared for the 1989 Beijing spring after Hu Yaobang's death. Therefore, though this protest was far greater in scale than the Democracy Wall Movement of ten years before, few were able to come up with any theory or tactics to direct the movement; there were no impressive slogans or essays or speeches, such as those that invigorated the Democracy Wall Movement in 1978.

What will be the party's next step? Deng recently called for the continuation of reform and open-door policies and for a new leadership, which is supposed to make people believe that "the situation is hopeful, reform is still being pursued." He has also called for those guilty of corruption to be punished, for "ten to twenty serious cases of corruption to be tried as showcases," as proof of the government's determination to deal seriously with the problem. But he has also been saying that the Four Principles are fundamentally sound, that if any problem exists, it is because they "have not been upheld thoroughly enough," and that the "suppression of bourgeois liberalism and spiritual pollution should be more actively undertaken."

After the massacre at Tiananmen Square, Deng and his clique lost the last shreds of the people's confidence. The nationwide wave of arrests has thrown the country into a white terror even more frenzied than during the Cultural Revolution. Even as Deng professes to want to continue reform policies and crack down on corrupt officials, he labels scholars and students "counterrevolutionary elements."

Since the Communist Party came to power, its authority has been absolute, encompassing every aspect of people's private lives. The rulers have refused to countenance any constitutionally guaranteed rights: freedom of the press, elections for people's representatives, an independent judicial process. They have refused all demands for people's supervision over the party, claiming that the party can correct its own mistakes. People may have believed such lies in the 1950s and 1960s, but subsequent decades have heightened their political consciousness, as the angry shouts of the hundreds of thousands on the Square testified.

After those bloody days, schisms within the party organization, from the highest level down to the grass roots, have become even more apparent. Many party members have publicly resigned, among them influential intellectuals. The control of the central leadership over local party organs, and the control of the local organization over its members, is greatly weakened. Party central has found out that in nearly all its subordinate organs, party cadres are covering up for activists in the democracy movement. As the leaders' impotence has become manifest, they find fewer and fewer people to trust, and they are resorting to increasingly fascist methods. Never before has the party taken such drastic or widespread measures to punish those they suspect of subversion, even people who have been loyal supporters and have given no grounds for suspicion. They have been stripped of their jobs, expelled from the party, arrested and sentenced to long terms in prison, permanently exiled to remote, uninhabited areas, and even executed.

Meanwhile, productivity has fallen drastically, and government departments are in a state of semiparalysis. Peasants have been refusing to sell their products because the state purchasing price is so low and the government often does not even have the cash to buy them. The government has discovered that guns can temporarily suppress a democratic movement but cannot solve pervasive economic and social problems.

The life expectancy of this government cannot be long. No one expects its successor to be a truly democratic one. Nor is it certain that it will abandon the self-destructive ways of the old men now ruling the country. But it is clear that the Chinese people are no longer lulled by disingenuous promises of reform. For three or four days after the Tiananmen Square massacre, university students in cities all over the country continued to demonstrate. The government crackdown gave birth to an underground resistance movement. In greater numbers and with renewed determination, the people will continue to organize and to pursue their struggle through both legal and nonlegal means.

The democracy movement that erupted in the spring of 1989 was far and away the largest China has ever known. Demonstrations took place in dozens of cities, even days after the June Fourth massacre. Unlike the student movements of the 1930s and 1940s, this latest uprising occurred spontaneously, independent of any political organization or leadership; yet it swelled to mammoth, record-breaking proportions. To be sure, the west has seen spontaneous student demonstrations in Europe and America in the 1960s, but conditions there differ from those in China, where the machines of oppression can roll down at any time and where virtually all urban adults are state employees. It takes real courage for someone to join a street demonstration in China.

Unlike the Chinese student demonstrations of 1985 and 1986–87, this most recent movement involved strong participation by intellectuals. Yet we hear criticism after criticism: "Not once during this movement did a truly inspired big-character poster appear!" "Not in the same league as the Democracy Wall Movement!" "Throughout the protest there was no war of words, nothing but 'Be resolute,' and no emphasis on tactics!" With intellectuals from several generations participating in one way or another, why were there no words, no strong leadership, no tangible supports?

One good answer is that no one anticipated such massive demonstrations. But how could this be? The student demonstrations in Beijing and elsewhere did not just happen—they were the inevitable consequence of long-standing crises in the nation. Intellectuals, especially those who study society and human relations, should not have been caught unprepared. The issue is whether intellectuals functioned during the democracy movement as they should have, and this issue is tied to the role they have played in the past.

Over the last decade, whenever you tried to interview an intellectual, you were always told, "I'm too busy." Manuscript deadlines, interminable meetings, too many people to see, and a long list of speaking engagements in China and abroad left no time for anything else. On closer examination, you would find that nearly all the articles, novels, and monographs were written for other intellectuals; in all the research, writing, discussions, and speeches, there was no direct reference to the real problems facing Chinese society. Circles of acquaintances were limited to intellectuals at one's own level. Everyone was wrapped up in economic, political, literary, or educational issues within a narrow field of specialization. Almost no one was occupied in research on current economic trends or political realities, China's rapidly worsening conditions, or shifts of power among social strata and political factions. As a result, a social scientist might be totally ignorant of major political events occurring in his own city.

As the state of Chinese society grew increasingly critical, the reaction of many intellectuals was to feel that democratization had become more distant than ever. The unprecedented inflation of 1988, the economic chaos created by bureaucratic profiteering, and the pervading sense of panic among the populace failed to instill any presentiments of the gathering storm. Quite the opposite, the intellectuals grew more pessimistic than ever. The pervading logic of the time was: since the prospects for democratization are so bleak, there is no need to get excited; forget everything but your own scholarly discipline.

But this sentiment was far removed from the realities of Chinese society. As early as 1985, galloping inflation and bureaucratic consolidation had given rise to widespread dissatisfaction. Violent protests erupted spontaneously in the countryside that year and quickly spread to the cities. Radical young intellectuals who could be held back no longer were itching for a fight, but they lacked leadership; some were even making preparations to form opposition parties. But in the upper levels of the party, the conservatives were on the attack, with Hu Yaobang in retreat, leading to such measures as the dismissal of the party secretaries in Fujian and Hainan Island, both ardent reformers.

A variety of causes, sometimes conflicting, led to a change in the relationship between intellectuals and society after 1979. The persecution of older and middle-aged intellectuals had finally come to an end, and they were allowed to return to their studies. The generation of intellectuals who had come to maturity during the Cultural Revolution were given the chance for further education and normal jobs, and were no longer forced to languish on the lowest rungs of the social ladder, as they had for so many years. At the same time, various subjective factors—a weary dis-

dain of politics, a blind faith or a total loss of faith in the leadership of the Communist Party, or disillusionment with life itself
and complete despair where China's future was concerned—
gradually caused the intellectuals to abandon interest in, ob-
servation of, and involvement in social life; they chose either to
remain ignorant of developments among the lowest levels of
society and within the Communist Party or to divorce themselves
from those developments. The excessive optimism over prospects of reform before 1984 and the excessive pessimism over
prospects of democratization after 1985 stem from this process of
distancing.

The years 1987 and 1988 are particularly significant, for it
was during this period that problems within Chinese society and
the Communist Party reached their critical peak, as discontent
and indignation among the people became more pronounced.
But many intellectuals, seeing only what was going on at the
highest level or superficial indications elsewhere (the forced res-
ignation of Hu Yaobang, the quelling of student demonstrations,
the prevailing bleak mood among the people), arrived at pessimistic conclusions, blind to the growing vitality brewing at all
levels of society. How could they have anticipated or prepared
for a democracy movement in 1989?

That brings us to the events of April 1989: the students boasted
of their independence, rejecting influence from any quarter (not
all of them, of course, were so resolute), while the intellectuals
could offer nothing that might serve the students. Their under-

standing of the workers, peasants, party and governmental cadres, even the students, was too limited.

The latest repressions in China can easily give rise to even more pessimism. But the situation resembles nothing less than a pressure cooker building up steam. What worries me is that the intellectuals will once again be unprepared for the next outburst of democratic sentiment that is sure to come.

The business in Beijing that remained unfinished in the spring of 1989 was continued in the fall in Eastern Europe, where changes far more spectacular than anything demanded by the students in Tiananmen Square were wrought in every Communist-ruled country except Albania. Ever since the first popular revolt in Eastern Europe nearly forty years ago, a number of uprisings— some violent, some peaceful—have demanded the world's attention; but none was successful. This phenomenon created the illusion that Communist regimes, wherever they were established, were so solidly entrenched that they could weather any storm. In China, moreover, the primary cause of a defeatist attitude among the people has been the absence of any organized political force in which they can place their hopes; a lack of options has made the overthrow of the Communist regime even less likely. But the drastic changes in Eastern Europe in 1989 had to remove that barrier in the minds of the Chinese.

With the exception of Poland, where Solidarity was already in existence, the people in the other countries did not have viable political organizations and were forced to organize themselves in the course of overthrowing the old regimes. In China, in addition to misconceptions regarding the Communist Party itself, another major psychological barrier can be summed up in the saying, "The leg is thicker than the arm, so how can you topple the powerful Communist Party?" Developments in Eastern Europe answered a question of great relevance to China: do the people, in the final analysis, have the courage to act? In only a few short days, the Romanian people neatly stripped Nicolae Ceausescu of power. In addition to the close ties long established between Romania and China, the two nations are remarkably similar: both are poor, neither has enjoyed democratic traditions or freedom of speech under their Communist regimes, and both had no experience in prerevolutionary political organization. By December 1989, Ceausescu had held power longer than any other Eastern European leader; his control appeared absolute after almost a quarter century, and his security apparatus was far more effective than anything in China. Unlike the other Eastern European countries, his nation had enjoyed decades of peace without Soviet intervention, and even though his people were living under economic conditions far harsher than those in China over the past several years, he encountered no strong resistance. On the face of it, the Romanian Communist regime was stronger than the Chinese regime.

The Chinese Communist Party had two distinct advantages

over the Romanian party: over the past decade, Romania's economic difficulties were without parallel in China; and China's geographical isolation has exposed it to fewer outside influences. Nonetheless, the Chinese democracy movement has at least one advantage over Romania: the decade-long Cultural Revolution and the last ten years of economic reforms have seriously weakened party unity and the party's domination over society. The people have become less and less dependent on the central government; meanwhile they have had a taste of freedom (especially economic freedom), which in turn has led to rising expectations and rapidly increasing demands for political freedom and democracy. The earlier Tiananmen Incident of 1976, the 1978–79 Democracy Wall Movement, and the three nationwide student movements since 1985 were clear reflections of this.

And yet the Chinese failed where the Romanians succeeded. Why?

Ceausescu's fall is particularly significant in China, for he was the closest foreign ally of the Deng regime. He firmly resisted the Gorbachev-led wave of reforms and was the only leader in Eastern Europe to send a congratulatory telegram to Deng Xiaoping after the June Fourth massacre in Beijing. By the time the other Eastern European nations had changed hands, Romania was still a pillar of support for Deng abroad. His existence served as proof that Deng's policy of "My path is the correct one" extended beyond China's borders.

That is why news of the success of Romania's revolution

produced such shock waves throughout China. From Beijing to Hong Kong, the news spread like wildfire amid an air of celebration; in Hong Kong, people even began buying strings of firecrackers in preparation for the day when Deng Xiaoping, Li Peng, and Yang Shangkun would fall from power. Many Chinese in China and abroad who were so pessimistic over prospects in China and Hong Kong began to take heart.

But the most significant impact of the changes in Eastern Europe, and Romania in particular, has been felt within party, government, and military circles. The octagenarians and diehards have reacted to the spectacular changes in Eastern Europe by offering them up as the strongest argument in support of Deng's thesis, "Never yield an inch, for retreat can only spell doom." Just look, they say, how all those Communist countries fell like dominoes. They are pounding this message into members of the bureaucracy, trying to rally the growing number of vacillators around them. But even some of the most obstinate diehards, especially their own sons and daughters, could not fail to see what Romania has proved: while concessions may guarantee the collapse of a regime, holding the line or stepping up the degree of suppression lead to the same result, with perhaps even more dire consequences. The European Communist parties that made concessions before it was too late retained a measure of influence in their countries' political structure, and they may conceivably rally their forces and regain the people's trust. The Romanian Communist Party, on the other hand, was utterly destroyed, and the party boss and his wife died in front of a firing squad.

Deng and his clique have always been extremely worried about the possible impact on China of the liberalization processes going on in Eastern Europe and the Soviet Union. Since 1985 news about Gorbachev's political reform has been very carefully shielded from the Chinese people. And now who would expect that, after the dramatic changes in its sphere of control, the Soviet Union is actually proclaiming advocacy of a multiparty system! This piece of news is like, as the Chinese saying goes, spilling oil on fire. It shocked the Beijing authorities even more than the news from Romania. The Soviet Union is the first socialist country in the world, its party the orthodox Marxist-Leninist party. If the Soviet party is to abandon its monopoly of power, then how can the Chinese party leadership expect submission from the Chinese people? Deng is in a dilemma: of course he would very much like to launch an anti-revisionism campaign, such as Mao launched some thirty years ago. But how many followers can he collect? Probably not one hundredth of those Mao could reach in the sixties. Moreover, the policies he himself has advocated since 1979 are exactly what Mao used to call "revisionism." Finally, in order to criticize Gorbachev, Deng must first let the Chinese people know what Gorbachev's revisionism is all about. In doing so, he risks the danger of the people's applause rather than the criticism he is after.

"Is Marxism-Leninism truly dead?" "Is all hope for the party lost?" "Can a popular revolt succeed with no organization and no leadership?" Doubt about how to answer these three questions for China was the main reason why party moderates adopted a wait-and-see attitude for so long before finally throwing in their lot with the octagenarians. But the questions have been better answered by recent events in Eastern Europe and the USSR, and many of these middle-of-the-roaders can now see a justification for siding with the democratic faction.

Members of the democratic faction within the party—those individuals who are fed up with government corruption, have given up on the Deng clique, and are willing to join the fight for democratization—can be found at every level; their numbers far exceed those of the diehards. They are just waiting for the right moment, waiting for the people to exert greater pressure on the party even as they themselves exert greater pressure within the party; they also hope to widen the gap between the party and the military. The transformation of Eastern Europe will doubtless bolster the confidence and determination of these people, who will work with increased vigor within the party and elsewhere. Quite possibly, they are already organizing themselves in certain regions and agencies, in preparation for a showdown.

Obviously Eastern Europe is but one factor, and an external one at that. Yet there is no lack of fuel beneath China's own political fires. Many Chinese have begun to mull over the results of the 1989 democracy movement, which showed how powerful they could be and how marked the divisions in the upper levels of the party and the government had become. They have also seen that the military is no longer the handy tool of Deng and his cohorts, and that China, unlike Romania, does not have a corps of rabidly loyal security police willing to lay down their lives for the ruler.

The Romanian revolution was launched when Ceausescu's troops opened fire on demonstrators in the city of Timisoara. Prior to December 17, few of Romania's citizens could have predicted that the people would rise up to overthrow the Ceausescu regime or that they would succeed in a period of only ten days. No one could have predicted that a month and five days after Ceausescu was unanimously reelected as party leader at the November 20 party congress, he would meet his end in front of a firing squad. But the conditions that assured the success of the Romanian revolution were no doubt years in preparation. Similar conditions exist in China, building up steam, and the results may be the same; it is just a matter of time.

The democratic activist and philosopher Hu Ping wrote recently in an article from his exile in America: "It is a virtual certainty that in the inner sanctum of the Chinese Communist Party, which has never known tranquility, a great many intrigues, good and evil, are urgently being carried out in secret. It is distinctly possible that in the coming months and years, dramatic or drastic changes will occur overnight."

That, however, will only be a beginning. The tyrants of China are no more merciful than their Romanian counterparts, and the Chinese may have to pay a price hundreds of times greater than the Romanians have already paid. And even if Deng Xiaoping and the octagenarians were to relinquish their political power, that would only be the first step on the long road toward solving China's problems.

INDEX

Albania, 139
Antibourgeois campaigns. *See* Bourgeois
    liberalization; Rightists

Bai Hua incident (1981), 88
Ba Jin, 37, 46, 51
Banquets, 77
Beijing: bureaucracy, 74; foreign corre-
    spondents, 95; after Hu Yaobang's
    death, 129; inflation, 3–4; small enter-
    prises, 106; Tiananmen massacre,
    121–122, 130, 135–136
Beijing Daily, 95
Beijing University, 29, 95; Public Opinion
    Institute of, 99–100
Bin county, 67–68
Bing Xin, 37
Birth rate, 104
Bourgeois liberalization, xiv–xxi, 8, 29,
    39–40, 45, 92, 123, 126
Bo Yibo, 126
Brezhnev, Leonid, xxi, 104–105
Budget deficit, 7
Bureaucracy, 34–35, 59; corruption,
    16–18, 66–69, 74–77, 78–79; de-
    fended by Central Committee, 20–21;
    economic power, 10–14; "moral and
    political emasculation," 63–65; under
    party, 61–62; size, 9, 70–72; strikes
    against, 54
"Bureauprof" (bureaucratic profiteering),
    14, 16–18, 74, 99
"Buying power of social groups," 10–11,
    77

Cadres, 61, 63, 68, 73
Capitalism, 26–27
Ceausescu, Nicolae, 140, 141, 145
Censorship, 84–86, 88
Central Committee of Communist Party,
    30; bureaucracy defended, 20–21; cen-
    sorship, 85; directives, 35; discipline,
    63; freedom of press reduced, 89; open
    letters to, 108; political reforms an-
    nounced, 18–19; rehabilitation, 87–88;

weakening prestige, 115; Zhao Ziyang
    removed, 117
Chen Yun, 79, 85, 96, 126
China Central Television (CCTV), 83–84
China Youth Daily, xv, 29–30, 89
Civil War (1948), 5–6
Cixi county, 68
Communist parties (Eastern Europe),
    142–143
Communist Party (Chinese): anti-intellec-
    tualism, 36, 45; attitudes toward,
    23–24, 52–53; and bureaucracy, 59,
    61–63, 72, 75–76; changes in, 27, 53,
    84; corruption in, 69, 73–75, 79; East-
    ern European parties and, 140–141;
    factions, 24, 27, 144; freedom under,
    29–30; on human rights, 108–109; and
    intellectuals, 40–45, 50, 138; under
    Mao, 54; May Fourth Movement and,
    34; newspapers on, 89–93; oppor-
    tunists in, 65–66; organizations under
    control, 52; popular concessions, 127;
    Propaganda Department, 84–85; and
    reform, 19–21, 125; Soviet party com-
    pared with, 67, 105; stability of, 6–7;
    strikes against, 54; after Tiananmen
    massacre, 130–131; weakening of, 107,
    115
Communist Party (Romania), 142–143,
    145
Communist Party (Soviet Union), 23, 24,
    67, 105, 143
Competition, economic, 17
Confucianism, 25
Consumer goods, 4, 11, 13, 15, 77
Corruption, 16–18, 66–69, 73–75, 78,
    104; campaigns against, 76–77; Deng's
    campaign against, 129–130. *See also*
    Bureaucracy
Crime, 104, 123
Cultural Revolution, 9, 48, 50–51, 73,
    93, 118, 125, 137–138, 141
Currency devaluation, 8–9, 74
Czechoslovakia, xxi, 41